進化するトーキョー日本料理

DEN

The Evolving Tokyo-Japanese Cuisine

はじめに

日本料理を新しい世代のものにしたい、と思っています。

おいしいものが好きでレストラン巡りも大好き、でもクラシックな料亭や割烹は敷居が高い…と感じている20代、30代の方たちがいます。その一方、外国からはパリやミラノに行くのと同じ感覚で、グルメ目的のツーリストが東京を訪れています。とにかく、おいしくてステキな体験を求めてレストランを予約する方々です。

彼らにこそ、アプローチしたいのです。本格的なコースの日本料理を食べるのは初めてという方々に日本料理のファンになってほしい。

わたしたちは傳という店で、ビギナーや外国の方にもわかりやすい味、どなたにもストレートに響くおいしさ、ワクワク感を刺激する演出を追いかけてきました。伝統料理をベースにしていますが、ときに大胆にアレンジし、ユーモラスに表現します。堅苦しいルールや文学的な表現は抜きにして、おいしさと楽しさを率直に目指す「日本料理のトラットリア」になれたらいいと思っています。

いまは日本料理の進化に取り組んでいますが、最終目標は「伝統」です。10年後のわたしはスキッとした雰囲気の白木のカウンターの店で江戸風の、古典どまんなかの料理をつくっているつもりです。傳で日本料理に初めて出会ったお客さまと一緒に、つぎのステップで本物の伝統料理に進みます。そのために今があります。

Introduction

I hope to open the door of traditional Japanese cuisine to the new generation.

Ryotei or *kappo*-traditional style Japanese cuisine restaurants are both fine-dining as well as a salon for sophisticated adults. Consequently young gourmets in their twenties and thirties feel that *ryotei* and *kappo* are too elite for them, even though they enjoy going to other gastronomic restaurants. I am sorry if they miss the opportunity to experience the formal Japanese course-menu. At the same time Tokyo and Tokyo's high-end restaurants, like those of Paris and Milan, have welcomed Foreign gourmets. Their main reason for visiting Japan is seeking to sample first-hand the exclusive and unique dining culture.

We at DEN have experimented to develop menus that are appealing both to the first-time local young customer as well as the Foreigner. Our dishes, based on traditional Japanese cuisine but are straightforward and easy to understand and friendly. We often present the dishes imaginatively and with a sense of fun.

At DEN we encourage a more relaxed dining manner, we like our guests to enjoy the dishes without rules or metaphoric expression. DEN is our "Japanese Trattoria"—a warm and welcoming place serving genuine and tasty food.

My focus now is evolving Japanese cuisine, but my ultimate aim is "the tradition". I will engage with classic cuisine in a typical *kappo* style restaurant ten years from now. My intention, as I move through the next steps as a chef, is to bring those guests whose first encounter of Japanese cuisine was at DEN, with me. Challenging today—building tomorrow.

目次

撮影／天方晴子
デザイン／甲谷 一（Happy and Happy）
翻訳／毛利桜子
編集／木村真季

一、季節の前菜とお造り

1. Seasonal appetizers and sashimi

季節感 リアルに響く
Seasonal cuisine

開店当初、料理はアラカルトで提供していました。毎日通ってくださる方に昨日と重ならないもの、今日の天候や体調に合うもの…と試行錯誤の日々。少しずつ常連さんが増え、2年目からコース料理だけのお店になりました。

献立はその日の食材をみて決めます。定番の名物料理に季節料理を組み合わせておおよその流れを決めたら、あとはお酒を楽しみたい方、お腹がすいている方、いろいろ体験したい外国の方…それぞれに合わせて最終アレンジ。アラカルト時代の経験が臨機応変の土台です。

ここ数年、外国人のお客さまが増えました。グルメ目的で来日し、一週間の滞在中にあちこちの料亭や割烹に行く方が少なくありませんが、そこでよく聞かれるのが「日本料理店のメニューは、どこもみな同じ」という声。どこのお店でも春なら若竹の炊合せ、夏には鮎の塩焼きが出てきたよ、と。

日本料理の献立は一種の歳時記で、「この時期にこれを食べる」という型があり、今年もこれを食べたという満足がおいしさにつながる…と考えられてきました。でも、目の前のお客さまは実際に何を感じていらっしゃるか、そこを慮ることがおもてなしです。昨日よそで召し上がったなら別の体験をしていただきたいし、真夏でも肌寒い日なら温かさを前に出したい。

日本料理のテーマは昔も今も季節感ですが、現代のお客さまにリアルに響く季節感でありたいのです。日本料理の約束事は知らなくても、自然に季節を感じ取れる表現を探しています。

When I first started DEN I served a la carte dishes for the first year. Some guests were dining every night, so I tried to create different dishes every day for those guests, in order to satisfy them. Sometimes the dishes varied according to the weather or guest's health. Eventually, as the number of repeat guests increased I decided to introduce only set menus from the second year.

The menu of the day will depend on the ingredients sent from the local traders or producers on the day. Signature dishes are served daily, and I match them with seasonal dishes. The dishes are prepared according to the guest's needs—whether they're enjoying an alcoholic beverage or how hungry they are or if foreign guests are looking forward to a new experience. Their "expectation" varies, so I'll be ready for it. The experience of the first year prepared me to be flexible.

For the past five to six years, the number of foreign guests at our restaurant has increased. For most people, the purpose of their visit to Japan is gourmet food. During their stay, they will visit various formal and traditional Japanese restaurants. I'm frequently asked by them, "why do all high-end Japanese restaurants serve the same dishes?". Wherever they go, if in spring, they will be served with a dish of "bamboo shoots and *wakame*", in summer "salt-grilled *ayu*" and so on.

Classic Japanese cuisine menus are like a seasonal calendar. There are certain patterns to follow regarding when to eat what. This is an important part of our culture, but, what's more important to us is how the guest is feeling. I would like to serve our own style of a dish something different from other restaurants. A dish which suits the day's temperature and humidity, a dish that a foreign guest could distinguish the seasonal key elements.

The main theme of Japanese cuisine has always been and still is today "the sense of season" but we don't need to be constrained by classical customs. I'm always looking for a way to be creative in expressing seasonal blessings.

トマトのところてん

じゅんさい
パッションフルーツ
バジルシード
土佐酢ゼリー

フレッシュのトマトでところてんをつくりました。器
にはすの葉をのせて提供しています。葉に落とした
「露」はトマトの香りのする甘酢。これを器にすべり落
としてから箸をとっていただきます。

Tomato *tokoroten*

junsai, passionfruit, basil seed, *tosa*-vinegar jelly

This dish is *tokoroten* jelly noodles made with agar and tomato. I use
lotus leaf to cover the bowl. "Dew" made with tomato flavoured sweet
vinegar is dropped onto the leaf. The guest would taste a spoonful
of dew, then drop the dew into the bowl. Enjoy *tokoroten* with your
chopsticks.

ビーツの穴子挟み揚げ、
しそ風味

梅雨が明けると、穴子がおいしくなります。海の素材なのにどこか土の風味を感じるこの魚に、まさに土の香りのするビーツを組み合わせました。しその風味が両者をつなぎます。コースの頭の部分でちょっとつまむ、スナック感覚の一品です。

Deep-fried conger and beetroot,
shiso flavour

After rainy season, conger becomes tasteful with good fatty. Even though conger is a fish of the sea, it has a subtle aroma of soil, which matches with the aroma of beetroot and the flavour of the *shiso* leaf brings them together. This is a snack like dish, served at the beginning of a course meal.

はもかつ

塩すだち

はもは、東京の料理人にとって"ちょっと構えてしまう"魚です。京料理の夏の主役というイメージが強いからか…そんな思い込みは抜きにして、シンプルに素材に向かいましょう。これは肉厚のはもを揚げた、ハムカツならぬ、はもかつ。ビールと一緒にざくざくっと頬張れば、文句なくおいしい。夏のパワーを感じる気軽な一品です。

Hamo cutlet

lightly salted *sudachi* citrus

For cooks in Tokyo, *hamo*, pike conger is not a part of our daily ingredient. It has the image of being one of the main summer ingredients of Kyoto cuisine. I made it into a carefree, fun dish. Enjoy *hamo-katsu* (*hamo* cutlet) with a glass of beer and it's guaranteed to be a casual summer dish satisfying to the palate.

ミニうに丼
おろしわさび
海ぶどう

ねっとりと甘い日本のうには外国人グルメにも大人気
です。これはひとくちサイズのうに丼。ほんのひとく
ちのごはんに「生うに」と「うにのづけ」をたっぷり
と重ねています。まずは「づけ」だけを味わい、それ
からごはんと一緒に生うにを。「浜に打ち上げられたう
に」をイメージして、殻の周りに乾燥わかめや煮干パ
ウダーをあしらいました。

Urchin, small rice bowl
grated *wasabi*, "sea grape" seaweed

The rich sweetness of Japanese urchin is very popular with foreign
guests. A mouthful of rice is topped with "raw urchin" and "*zuke*
(marinated) urchin". Try the *zuke* first, then the raw urchin with rice.
The image of this dish is, "urchin washed away on the beach", garnish
around the shell with dried seaweed and dried fish powder.

山いもの昆布締め

たたきおくら
温泉卵

やまいもの素麺仕立て。テーマはずばり「ねばねば、ずるずる」。いかにも日本な夏のテクスチャーを、めんつゆ味でまとめました。

Japanese yam marinated with *kombu*

crushed okra, "*onsen*" poached egg

Cut Japanese yam in strips as thin as capellini noodles. The theme of this dish is "*neba-neba, zuru-zuru* ; sticky and slurping", one of the characteristic textures of a Japanese summer delight. This is served with basic *men-tsuyu* sauce.

うにと生ゆばの
べっこう餡
おろしわさび

Urchin and fresh *yuba*, "*bekko-an*" sauce
grated wasabi

「夏はあっさりした味で」と、だれしも思うものですが、あっさりばかりではもの足りない。べっこう餡は冬のあつあつ料理ですが、これを夏向けに仕立てました。かつおの香りをきりっときかせ、普通よりも少し甘めに味をつけています。暑い日に冷たくして、少し肌寒い日は温かくして提供します。生のとうもろこしを入れる別バージョンもあり。とうもろこしのフレッシュな甘みがうにのコクを引き立てます。

"Simple and light taste" is many people's preference in summer. But sometimes we want more than just light flavour. I arranged piping-hot winter "*bekko-an*" starchy sauce to be a dish enjoyed in summer. A sauce with the sharp aroma of *katsuobushi* and seasoned lightly sweet, served chilled on hot days and warmer on chilly days. Another version is adding raw corn: the fresh natural sweetness of the corn accentuates the richness of the urchin.

穴子の天ぷらとなすのお浸し
おくら餡
ぶぶあられ

穴子は揚げたてのほくほく。おくら餡は常温です。つ
るりとした餡の喉ごしが、穴子の香り、だしをたっぷ
り含んだなすの旨みを引き立てます。

Anago tempura and eggplant "hitashi"
okra sauce, small bits of rice cracker

Anago conger tempura is both crispy and fluffy. The smoothness
of okra-starchy-sauce enhances the aroma of conger and umami of
katsuo-dashi soaked eggplant.

きのこ豆腐

粟麩
赤こんにゃく
揚げぎんなん
ぶぶあられ

料理界きのこ部を自負する、わが傳チーム。毎年夏の終わりに、富士山麓にスタッフ総出できのこ狩りに出かけます。夏きのこも秋きのこも両方見つかるおもしろい季節で、年によってきのこの顔ぶれが微妙に変わるのも一興です。採れたての香りは時間勝負ですから、すべて一緒にすり流しにして葛で寄せ、揚げ出し豆腐に。もっちりした舌触りと揚げ出しのこくとともに「今年の秋」の香りを伝えます。

Mushroom "tofu"

awa-fu , *konjak*, ginkgo nut, rice cracker

We consider team DEN as "the mushroom club". Every year, at the end of summer, we visit the foot of Mt. Fuji to pick mushrooms. It's a unique time of the year when both summer and autumn mushrooms are found. It's interesting that depending on the year, the variety of the mushroom changes. Preserving the aroma of freshly picked mushroom is a race against time. For this dish, we puree all the mushrooms and form it into *tofu* with *kudzu*, and serve it deep-fried. A dish to enjoy the smooth, chewy-like texture and richness of deep-fried *tofu*, and the fragrance of "autumn".

本ししゃものフライ

本ししゃもは日本にのみ生息する魚で、食べられるのは1年のうちわずか2〜3週間。頭はカリッと香ばしく、身はほくほく、ヒレはパリパリ…に揚げて、繊細な風味を丸ごとストレートに味わっていただきます。

Deep-fried *hon-shishamo* smelt

Hon-shishamo is a fish only found in Japan. It can only be enjoyed two to three weeks in a year. Deep-fry the whole fish, head crisp, flesh soft and fin crunchy crispy. Enjoy the delicate flavour by savouring the whole fish.

グローバルな日本料理
Global Japanese cuisine

この数年、海外での出仕事が増えています。ヨーロッパ、北米、中南米、アジア…『傳』の料理を多くの人に味わってもらう機会です。同時に、私たち自身が海外のレストラン文化のありようを体感する機会でもあります。

友人からよく不思議がられるのですが、私は未知の土地で日本料理をつくるにあたって心配したことがありません。日本から持っていくのはかつお節、醤油、みりんくらい。あとはすべて現地で調達します。現地に着いたらまず市場に行って食材を知り、魚を調達して一夜干しにしたり、そのアラでだしを引いたり。ドライトマトをペーストにして味噌がわりに使うなど、異国ならではの工夫もします。日本料理のすべてが可能とは言いませんが、現地の素材を使い、日本料理的に解釈して、日本料理として表現することは可能です。できたものはオーセンティックではなくとも、グローバル時代の日本料理だと思っています。

外国の方は日本料理というと「繊細な盛りつけ」をまずイメージするようですが、そこにはあまりこだわりません。こだわりたいのは温度です。たとえば、ふわっと湯気があがるくらいの熱さ。それをハフハフしながらまずひとくち味わい、少し温度が下がったところをゆっくりと味わう。この「温度感」、とくに口の中を温度が通過していく感じが、日本料理のおいしさではないかと思うからです。そんなライブ感を大事にしています。

For the past several years I have often gone abroad to present my Japanese cuisine. It's an opportunity for me to introduce the taste of DEN in Europe, America and Asia. At the same time, I have been able to experience the overseas' restaurant culture.

My friends wonder why I don't feel anxious when serving Japanese cuisine in an unfamiliar country. I've never felt I needed to worry about anything. The only ingredients I'd bring from Japan are *katsuo-bushi*, soy sauce and *mirin*. The rest of the ingredients are procured locally. When I arrive at a destination, the first thing I would do is to visit the local market. I'd familiarize myself with the local produce and experiment with them, trying overnight drying or extracting dashi from locally available fish. I would improvise, for example, substituting dried tomato for *miso*. It is possible to create Japanese cuisine with the local ingredients. It may not be an authentic Japanese cuisine but I see it as a Japanese cuisine of the global era.

The foreigner's image of Japanese cuisine may be the delicate presentation of a dish, but for me the temperature of a dish is more important. Let me explain this further; When we serve a steaming hot dish I'd like the guest to first take in the fresh seasonal aroma. Then, taking the first mouthful, as the dish is piping-hot, and when the temperature settles, the guest will taste the differences in flavour. This "sense of heat" is one of distinctive features of Japanese cuisine. I'd really like guest to enjoy this changing temperature passing through their mouth and throat.

花びら酢がき

食用のベコニアには独特の酸味があり、シルキーな舌
触りやシャキシャキした歯切れもユニーク。料理にア
クセントを加えてくれる魅力的な食材です。ブラジル
でコラボレーションをしたシェフ、アレックス・アタ
ラ氏の「お花のセビーチェ」に触発されました。

Oyster in vinegar with flower petals

Edible begonia has a distinctive acidity, silky texture and crispiness.
An attractive ingredient that gives accent to this dish. I was inspired
by Chef Alex Atala's dish "Flower ceviche", with whom I collaborated
in Brazil.

えびいもの熟成焼き

むろで2〜3カ月熟成させたえびいもを蒸→煮→揚→焼…と調理します。皮は香ばしくて味が濃く、中は栗きんとんのようにねっとり。えびいもの個性を、極端に凝縮させています。落ち葉に見立てた茶葉の中からアツアツを掘り出し、焼きいものように手づかみで召し上がっていただく趣向です。

Roasted, matured *ebiimo* taro

I use *ebiimo* taro matured for two to three months. Then the dish is prepared in this order, steam→simmer→deep-fry→roast. The outside will have roasted richness, and the inside will be as smooth as chestnut paste. Sprinkle tea leaves on the top. Imagine digging out piping-hot *ebiimo* from autumn leaves. Serve it hand eating style.

かぶの風呂吹き

ゆず味噌餡

餡は、ゆず味噌を豆乳ベシャメルでのばしたもの。春先には木の芽味噌をベースにしてつくることもあります。仕上がりは「マイルドな田楽」のような「グラタン」のようなイメージ。味噌の濃厚さに慣れない外国の方にも無理なく親しんでいただけます。

Turnip, "*furofuki*" style

yuzu-miso sauce

Make the sauce with soy milk béchamel and *yuzu*-flavoured-*miso* (in early spring, I'd sometimes use *kinome*-flavoured-*miso*). Image it as "sweet and mild *miso* sauce". A dish that can be enjoyed even by foreigners who are not used to the richness of *miso*.

香箱がにの薬膳飯蒸し

蒸したての香箱がにを黒米の飯蒸しにのせて「お凌ぎ」にしました。松の実入りのおこわの香ばしさが、かにの風味を引き立てます。お凌ぎは必ず出すと決めているわけではなくその日の献立やお客さま次第ですが、コースの前半にほんの少量でもごはんやおこわの一品があると、女性や外国の方にとても喜ばれます。

Kobako-crab steamed with black rice

Place freshly steamed snow crab on top of steamed black rice. It's served as "*oshinogi*", a small dish, served as "a tiding over" until the next dish is served. The aroma of steamed sticky rice with pine nuts brings out the flavour of crab. "*Oshinogi*" is not a dish I served all the time, it depends on the day's menu and guests. A small rice dish served at the first half of the meal does have a positive impact on ladies and foreign guests.

傳の「お造り」には、つけ醤油の小皿がありません。お客さまが刺身を醤油にひたす、という行為は想定しないことにしています。かわりに、その魚に合わせたソースやガーニッシュで直接あえるか、あるいは添えることで、一品を完成させています。

本来、刺身とは食べる人が仕上げる料理で、「味の濃い」醤油を、魚に「ほどよく」つけることで完成します。でも、その適量が意外とむずかしい。慣れない外国の方は、つけすぎてしまいがちです。醤油味ばかりが勝てば、魚のおいしさは完全には伝わりません。ならば、最初から「たくさんつけてもおいしい醤油」を用意すればいい、という考え方なのです。あるいは、あらかじめ刺身を調味して味を完成させてもいい。

こうして「つけ醤油」から「ソース」へと発想を変えました。変えたことで、お造り自体にも広がりが出てきました。わたしのなかでお造りが前進しました。

ただし、そこで伝えたいものが日本の刺身文化であることに変わりはありません。テーマは「うまみ」と「歯ごたえ」です。魚の質を見極め、それにかなった熟成をさせることにあります。

最近は海外の料理業界でもイケジメということばが知られてきました。魚のクオリティに対する日本人の感性が世界じゅうの料理人を刺激しています。生産者、流通のプロ、料理人がひとつになって育ててきた目利きやテクニックを、刺身を通して伝えたいと思っています。

DEN's sashimi does not come with a small dish of soy sauce. The flavour of the sashimi is completed with the original sauce, or with garnish tossed or served on the side.

Sashimi is a dish, where seasoning is left up to the person eating the dish. This seasoning is by dipping sashimi into strong flavoured soy sauce. But dipping just the right amount can be tricky. Foreign guests sometimes use too much soy sauce. When your palate is overwhelmed by soy sauce, it's difficult to enjoy the flavour of the fish. So why not serve it with an creative sauce that doesn't need "quantity adjustment"? Better yet, complete the seasoning before serving the dish. By changing the style, it made me see new ways to present this traditional dish.

Even if the style changes, it doesn't change the fact that, "traditional Japanese sashimi culture" is important for me. The important theme here is "umami" and "texture". First, we need "the eyes" to see the quality of the fish, then we must mature it adequately.

In recent years, the word *ikejime* is known even in the overseas culinary scenes. The Japanese sensibility for quality of the fish is inspiring chefs worldwide. With the collaboration of producers, professional distributors and chefs, we have cultivated this technique and this makes sashimi satisfying to the palate. This is what I'd like to express in my sashimi dishes.

ぶり大根

脂ののったぶりを、うまみマックスになるまで熟成させてから、づけに。極薄ビーツの甘酢漬けを「がり」の感覚で重ねます。ビーツの酸味とカリカリが、ぶりのねっとり感と好対照になって、パワフルな旨みの中の繊細な味わいを引き立てます。酸味には旨みを際立たせる効果があり、とくに外国の方に喜ばれます。昆布だしに梅干しを入れるようなもので、旨みをわかりやすく伝えてくれるようです。

Yellowtail and beetroot

Use fatty yellowtail. Mature it until umami is maximized, then marinate it for a short time in soy based sauce. Arrange, sweet pickled beetroot thinly sliced like "*gari*" and yellowtail, on top of each other. Enjoy the contrast of crisp vinaigrette *gari*-beetroot and the moist texture of yellowtail. I think the acidity accentuates the sensitive flavour of umami.

鰆のたたき
海苔酢

醤油ではなく、生海苔をソースにしました。酢をきか
せて海苔の風味を立たせることがポイントです。ヒン
トはお鮨の巻きもの。ネタ・海苔・酢飯…あの絶妙な
バランスです。この海苔酢なら、魚にたっぷりつける
ことができます。海外でも乾燥海苔を使ってつくれま
すが、外国には「黒いものは食べない」方もいるので、
酸味をつけた野菜のガーニッシュに代えることもあり
ます。

Seared Spanish mackerel
nori-vinegar sauce

In place of soy sauce, I made a sauce with raw *nori* seaweed for
this dish of sashimi. The key ingredient is vinegar. An appetizing
combination of fish, *nori* and vinegar is just like *"maki-sushi"*. Even
with plenty of sauce, it won't masque the flavour of sashimi. When
preparing overseas, use dried *nori*. For those who prefer not to eat
black food, I'd sometimes substitute it with vinegared vegetable as
a garnish.

さんまの肝あえ

とびこ
青ねぎ
炒りごま

Pacific saury with liver sauce
flying fish roe, chive, toasted sesame

This sauce is made with a combination of saury liver and *miso*. Because of its strong flavour, it's good with *sake*. Adjust the quantity of sauce, for non-drinking guests. Sometimes I would serve it with rice (vinegared rice with *myoga* ginger, *shiso* and sesame). When serving this dish to foreign guests, we explain that for Japanese, "if the liver is not eaten, then you'll be only getting half the value of a saury".

さんまの肝に味噌を合わせたソースは、お酒の進む濃い目の味なので、お酒を飲んでいないお客さまには少なめに按配しています。下にごはん（みょうが、大葉、ごまをのせた酢飯）を敷くことも。外国人のお客さまには「さんまは、肝を食べないと価値が半分」という日本のこだわりを申し添えて、提供します。

あおりいか
インパクト

フルール・ド・セル

大きく分厚いあおりいかを熟成させ、軽く塩をして甘みを引き出します。舌だけでなく、口の全体で味わえるよう、少し大きめの切りつけで。

Aori squid impact
fleur de sel

To bring out the sweetness of large and thick *aori* squid, salt it lightly and mature for several days. Cut the squid into large pieces, each mouthful will be satisfying to the palate.

熟成くろむつの土佐醤油あえ

脂ののったくろむつを、表面がねっとりするくらいまで熟成させています。フレッシュな魚の場合は歯ごたえを意識してやや薄めに切りますが、熟成させた魚は、少し厚めに切り出して口の中全体で味わっていただきます。もちもちした触感の合間から、旨みがじわじわと広がります。

Japanese bluefish with *tosa-soy-sauce*

Mature the fatty bluefish until it has a sticky moist texture and cut it into thick slices to fully enjoy. Umami will slowly spread in your mouth.

初がつお

わさびの茎の醤油漬け
わさびの花
おろしわさび

前日夕方の漁で釣れたかつおを、翌夜にお造りに。初夏のかつおならではの、清新な香りと歯ごたえが主役です。つけ醤油を添えるかわりに、わさびの茎の醤油漬けをまとわせました。わさびの茎と花もこの時季だけのもの。それぞれ根とは異なる香りがあり、風味が軽やかにふくらみます。

Early summer bonito

wasabi stems marinated in soy sauce,
wasabi blossoms, grated *wasabi*

Bonito caught in the evening will be sashimi the next night. Early summer bonito has a clean and fresh aroma and a texture unique to this season. Instead of soy sauce, I garnish it with soy marinated *wasabi* stems. *Wasabi* stems and blossoms are also seasonal ingredients. Each has a distinctive aroma and flavour that gives a refreshing impression.

すずきの造り

塩すだち

刺身1枚1枚の厚さをあえて不ぞろいに。歯ごたえの違いが出て、より立体的に味わえます。塩すだちのほのかなえぐみもアクセント。食用花のベゴニアの酸味と乾いた舌触りも新鮮な印象です。魚に脂がのっている場合は、少し醤油をぬります。

Sea bass sashimi

lightly salted *sudachi* citrus

Cut the sea bass fillet into uneven pieces to enjoy the texture. Lightly salted *sudachi* citrus adds subtle bitterness. Begonia's (edible flower) silky texture and acidity will leave a fresh impression on the palate. When preparing sea bass with a lot of fat, brush on a small portion of soy sauce.

刺身と刺身を混ぜる

Sashimi + sashimi

複数の魚を混ぜた刺身、という発想があってはいけないでしょうか。

本来は、AならAという魚の個性をストレートに味わう料理です。そのために最高の素材を求め、技術を尽くすのですから、ここに別の魚Bを混ぜたら、意味不明になります。

でも現実には、主役級の魚がいつもあるわけではありません。端境期もあれば、天候のせいで魚種が少なかったり、魚に脂がのっていない日もあります。最高のAを出すことを唯一の目的にすると、理想のAがない日は妥協するしかありません。海外の出仕事ではなおさらです。外国で自分のディナーを供する場合は、素材はすべて地元で調達しますが、食文化も流通事情も異なる土地で日本と同じ理想を求めるとしたら、そもそも無理があります。

では、素材頼みの発想を変えたらどうでしょう。ソロで主役を張る力がなければ、ほかの魚と混ぜてお造りにしたらどうでしょう。互いの足りないところを補って、相乗効果のおいしさが生まれるポイントを探ります。脂ののった魚といか、えびと貝、まぐろの赤身と牛サーロイン…混ぜ造りにすると、思いがけないおいしさが生まれます。

「素材自身の個性を引き出す」刺身の技術に、「恣意的に味をつくる」という西洋料理的な発想を加味すると、新しい世界が開けるのではないかと感じています。

Is it wrong to mix different types of fish to create a sashimi dish?

Sashimi is a dish where you enjoy the distinctive flavour of a fish. We look for a fish with the finest quality and employ our best techniques to bring out its characteristics. So mixing another type of fish just blurs the distinctive character we are seeking.

In reality we're not always able to prepare with a fish that can play the "main role", because fish can be scarce in between seasons, or only small catches due to bad weather, or days when we just can't find fish with good fat. This can often be the case when working overseas. When I prepare dinner in a foreign country I'd procure the ingredients locally. I find that with the difference in fish consuming culture and the distribution system, it's impossible to ask for the same kind of standard as that of Japan.

If I look for a fish to play the "main role", when I can't find it, I'd have to compromise with what is available. So why not change the concept of one fish as the "main role", and prepare mixed sashimi with two or three fishes. This way, I can find a way to create a dish by making up for what is lacking with one fish with another fish. For example, fatty fish with squid, shrimp with shellfish, red tuna with beef sirloin. These mixed sashimi bring out unexpected delicious flavours. This is another way to enjoy sashimi.

The concept of Japanese cuisine, "bringing out the character of the produce" combined with the occidental philosophy of "being original and creative". This has inspired me to have a new outlook for a sashimi dish.

いさきと鯵の混ぜ造り

みょうが
花穂紫蘇

あじは脂は少なめですが、香りが豊か。いさきは歯ご
たえがあって、この日は脂ののりも上々。それぞれ細
切りにして、土佐醤油であえ混ぜにします。混ぜるこ
とで、香り、旨み、歯ごたえが充実したハーモニーが
生まれます。土佐醤油にすだちを加えて酸味を立たせ
る仕上げもあります。その日のコースのバランスをみ
て、どちらかに

Grunt and horse mackerel
myoga ginger, *shiso* blossom

Horse mackerel is a fish with little fat, but is rich in aroma. Grunt has
fine texture and today's catch is fatty. Cut both fish into thin strips and
dress it with *tosa-soy-sauce*. By mixing both fish, it makes an excellent
harmony of aroma, umami and texture. Depending on the course
menu of the day, add *sudachi* citrus to *tosa-soy-sauce* for extra acidity.

二、名物をつくる

2. Our signature dishes

1 フォワグラ最中

コースの最初の一品として、必ずお出しするのがこの最中です。

具のフォワグラはブランデーでマリネするかわりに、西京漬けにして火入れしています。一緒に挟む添えものは、甘みのある季節の素材のペーストとお漬けもの。甘みと塩気、カリカリの歯ごたえと最中の皮の香ばしさがフォワグラを引き立てます。

西洋素材をメインで使うことはじつはほとんどないので、このフォワグラは例外です。あえて使うのは、フォワグラなら世界中のグルメに説明なしに通じるから。お箸が不要なのもストレスフリーです。最初に見て「え、何これ？」とちょっとびっくり、袋を開けるときにワクワク。食べてみての印象はたしかに日本料理で、そのうえ最中という日本のお菓子文化も紹介できる──小さなひとくちに、これらすべての思いを込めています。

席について最初に出てくる料理が、必ずこれであることが肝心です。「うちのお店は、こういうスタイルですよ」という、名刺がわりのようなもの。日本のおいしさを、どうぞリラックスして楽しんでください、というメッセージです。

料理に込める思いはいろいろあっても、ことばで説明するものではないと思っています。ありのままに食べて楽しみ、トータルに感じていただけたらベストです。

ご挨拶がわり
フォワグラ最中

As a greeting;
Foie gras *monaka*

Monaka is a Japanese traditional sweet with red bean paste sandwiched between wafers made from sticky rice.

I always serve foie gras *monaka* as a first dish of my course meal. Instead of marinating foie gras with brandy, it's marinated with sweet *miso*. We sandwich foie gras with the paste of naturally sweet seasonal ingredients and Japanese pickle between *monaka* wafers. Sweetness, saltiness, crunchiness, and the toasted aroma of *monaka* wafers bring out the flavour of foie gras.

I rarely use occidental ingredients to play the main role, so using foie gras is an exception. Why do I use it? because foie gras is known to gourmets worldwide and requires no explanation.

This is stress free easy to eat dish, chopsticks are not required.

When guests see it for the first time, I receive reactions like "what is this?" then they have fun opening the little package. When they bite into it, they will definitely taste a Japanese dish. A lot of what I'd like to express is in this small package.

So, it's important that this is the first dish, when guests are seated at the table. This is like a greeting message that says "this is our style, so please relax and enjoy".

I hope that instead of words the meal itself, the total experience of it, will communicate what we want to express to guests.

白いんげん豆
奈良漬け

White kidney beans
Narazuke pickle

きざみ干し柿
いぶりがっこ

Chopped dried *kaki*
Smoked & dried *daikon* pickle

干しいも
新しょうが甘酢漬け

Semi-dried sweet potato
Sweet vinegared young ginger

栗の渋川煮
しば漬け

Simmered chestnut with astringent skin
Shibazuke pickle

フォワグラは、白味噌ベースの漬け床で約1週間マリネします。期間は季節に応じて。湯煎で加熱した後、棒状に切り出し、形を整えてから切り分けます。

Marinate foie gras in sweet *miso* for one week (change the marinating period depending on the season). Take it out of *miso* and cook in a bain-marie. Cool it, shape into a stick and slice it into pieces.

日本にしかない食材、日本料理でしか味わえないおいしさは数多ありますが、日本料理初体験の人にそのすべてが伝わるとは限りません。知識として楽しめたとしても、味覚的に純粋に楽しめている？　おいしさは心に残っている？——このことをいつも考えています。

外国人のお客さまにも伝わりやすい、インパクトを与えられる食材とは何なのでしょう。もちろん日本人のお客さまにとっても、おいしく、晴れがましくひとときを楽しめる食材で。

すっぽんは日本独特のミステリアスな食材であり、その力強くすっきりとしたスープの旨みは誰にとってもわかりやすいおいしさです。だしを仕込んでおけば、シンプルでバリューな1品にできるところも魅力。

というわけで1年を通して、すっぽん料理を毎日扱っています。料理の基本形となるのが、この「お椀」。傳では、いわゆる一番だしのお椀を出さないので、そのかわりという意味もありますが、主役然した一品ではなく、「口替り」的な小椀としてコースの合間に挟みます。具はごく軽く、たとえば夏はにゅうめんでさっぱり塩味。冬は焼き餅を入れて、醤油味に…といった具合いです。

蓋のかわりにきれいに洗って乾かした甲羅をのせます。すっぽん初体験の方に「スペシャルなものを食べた」という印象が残るよう、グロテスクになりすぎないよう…ぎりぎりの演出。お客さまが「え？」と驚いたところで、食材の種明かしをいたします。

There are ingredients that are only found in Japan, and flavours that can only be enjoyed as Japanese cuisine. I often wonder if the palate of people who experience authentic Japanese cuisine for the first time is truly satisfied? Was the taste memorable? Or was it just an interesting experience?

What is an ingredient that is easy to understand and has impact on foreign guests? Preferably, an ingredient that can also be enjoyed as a special meal for Japanese guests.

Suppon is an ingredient unique to Japan and also somewhat mysterious. Strong and clean umami of *suppon* broth is straightforward and delicious. *Suppon* broth can be turned into simple but exceptional dishes.

This is the reason why I cook with *suppon* all year around. The standard dish for this ingredient is *suppon* soup. At DEN, we don't serve "*owan* soup", an extra-fine dashi soup. Instead, we serve *suppon* soup at an interval of course a meal. A small bowl of soup with minimum ingredients, for example, *somen* noodle in salt seasoned soup in summer, grilled *mochi* (rice cake) in soy seasoned soup in winter.

For a lid, we use cleaned turtle shell. It's important to impress guests with "something special", but we're careful not to make it too grotesque looking. When guests have a questionable look on their faces and react with "what?" only then we explain what it is.

すっぽんと
松茸のスープ

Suppon softshell turtle consommé with *matsutake*

すっぽん雑炊

お客さまの口から今日は少し体調悪い…、病み上がり
で…ということばがあったときには、こんな展開も。
すっぽんだしがあれば、軽い食事としてさっとおつく
りできます。

Suppon zosui

When guests let us know that they're feeling under the weather or
have just gotten over an illness, we can quickly prepare a light meal
with very nutritious *suppon* broth.

すっぽんのおこげ

すっぽんスープには、肉のだしと同レベルの強さがあるので、中華風の仕上げによく合います。いろいろな展開ができそうです。この野菜あんには油はいっさい使っていませんが、油を使っているかのようなコクがあり、しかも後味はキレよく、すっきり。そこがすっぽんの強みです。

Suppon and *okoge*, deep-fried crispy rice

Suppon broth flavour is as strong as meat broth. It's great with a Chinese style dish and we have turned it into a variety of dishes. This vegetable *an* sauce, baced on *suppon* broth even if oil is not used in cooking, is rich in flavour as though oil has been used, and the after taste is refreshingly clean. That is the distinctive characteristic of *suppon*.

すっぽんまんじゅう

寒い日につくりたくなる「ほかほかのすっぽんまん」。
中華の肉まんからのアレンジで、醤油味をきかせたすっ
ぽんの餡を肉まんの皮（すっぽんに見えるよう、竹炭で
黒くしています）で包んでいます。

Suppon manju, steamed buns

On a cold day, I like to make these "piping-hot *suppon* buns". It's a
variation of Chinese meat buns. Buns filled with seared *suppon*
meat and sticky rice seasoned with soy sauce. We make black buns,
coloured with bamboo charcoal to resemble *suppon*.

すっぽんラーメン

すっぽんだしに、具は野菜オンリー。中華麺は知り合いのお店につくってもらっているもので、二日間熟成させてから使います。しっかりのごはん料理は入らないけれど少しだけ何かを、という方向けに。ラーメンは外国人ゲストには驚くほど喜ばれます。

Suppon ramen

Ingredients are simple, *suppon* broth and vegetables. Chinese noodles are specially made and aged two days at a friend's shop. This ramen is for those too full for a rice dish, but want something light. Ramen is a popular dish for foreign guests.

3 デンタッキー

　フライドチキン？テイクアウト？　箱の中は「日本料理の手羽餃子」です。鶏の手羽に飯蒸しなどの具を詰めて揚げたもの。お凌ぎとしてコース半ばで出しています。

　ジョークまじりのプレゼンテーションもそうですが、手づかみでむしゃむしゃ食べるスタイルも日本料理らしからぬところ。開業2年目の年末に、クリスマスはチキンでしょう、と参鶏湯をアレンジした手羽餃子を出したことが最初でした。さらにファストフードをパロディにした紙箱に入れたら、外国人にも説明不要で通じるところがツボにはまったのか、予想外の反響に。SNSへのアップが相次いで、年じゅう「あれないの？」といわれるようになりました。

　パロディ部分ばかりが注目されがちですが、ふざけているわけではなく、紙箱には「蓋もの」のイメージを重ねています。うちのメニューにはお椀がないのでそのかわりに。お客さまが蓋に手をかけ、パッと開けて、まず香りと光景を楽しむ…そのワクワク感は、蓋付きの食器を使う日本料理ならではのものだからです。

　クスッと笑ったり、脱力したりしながら箱をあけ、手づかみでパクッとかじる。香ばしいチキンの中の具は、季節ごとに変わります。おいしさとユーモア、気楽さと日本料理らしさをそれぞれに込めています。

あかざえびと木の芽
Langoustine with *kinome* bud of Japanese pepper

黒米の薬膳飯蒸し
Sticy black rice with *yakuzen* ingredients

スパイシー飯蒸し
Spicy sticky rice with almond

インカポテトと黒トリュフ
"Inka" potato with black truffe

Dentucky

Fried chicken? To go? Open the box and find "Japanese chicken wing dumpling". Deep-fried chicken wing stuffed with ingredients, presented like a little joke and a dish to eat with your hands. This is not a typical Japanese cuisine style. It all started on the second Christmas of the restaurant, "It's Christmas, so we'll serve chicken!"

Korean chicken ginseng soup was transformed into chicken wing dumplings. We served it in a paper box as a parody to a fast food restaurant. We received an unpredicted amount of reactions to this dish. It seemed as though no explanation was necessary, even for the foreign guests to understand what we wanted to say. It was repeatedly uploaded on SNS. Guests asked for it all year around "do you have it today?"

The humorous part of this dish is often featured, but actually the paper box with the lid represents "*futamono*". *Futamono* is a dish served with a lid, typically served as a bowl of extra-fine *dashi* soup. The anticipation of opening a lid and finding what's inside then enjoying that first aroma, is a traditional Japanese cuisine style of serving with a lid. You may chuckle a little as you casually open this box. Pick up the chicken with your fingers and bite into it. The ingredients inside the crispy chicken will change depending on the season. In this box the guest will find the essence of a Japanese cuisine dish served with a sense of humour and seasonal deliciousness.

鶏は朝挽きのもの。手羽に具を詰め、小麦粉をまぶして揚げ、最後に上火オーブンに入れてパリッと仕上げます。
Stuff the chicken wings with the ingredients. Dredge in flour and deep-fry. Heat it in a salamander until the skin is crispy.

季節のサラダ

　日本料理の野菜の価値を上げたい、という思いがあります。野菜の旨みを使いこなしたい。コースの華になるような野菜料理をつくりたい。

　サラダは、この店でコースメニューをはじめたときから取り組んでいる料理です。最初の頃を思い出すと、9年前は半分の人が残していました。とにかく、日本のおじさんはサラダを食べません。生野菜がきらい？どうしたら野菜ひとつひとつを大事に味わい、おいしく食べてもらえる？…結局のところ、日本料理らしいサラダとは何か、なのです。

　野菜自体の個性は、欧米やアジアのそれと比べてむしろ弱め。ならば、そのデリケートさを突き詰めます。野菜ひとつひとつに応じたアプローチで調理して、それぞれの存在感を引き出す。煮る、ゆでる、浸す、揚げる、酢漬け…。揚げるにしても野菜それぞれで温度帯が異なります。葉もの1枚、なすひと切れ、ひとつひとつに、繊細に手間をかけています。

　今は20～30種類の野菜を使っています。何を使うかは、当日朝届いたものを見て決める。千葉の農家に嫁いだ姉がつくってくれる青菜や根菜類は強い味方です。盛り合わせたらやさしい個性の白絞油を少量かけるだけで、酢は使いません。ほんの少しの塩昆布をトッピングして旨みをプラスします。

　できあがりの見た目から、ミッシェル・ブラスのガルグイユの和食版？と聞かれることもありますが、いえいえ、むしろ日本料理に昔からある「炊き合わせ」の仕事です。野菜をそれぞれ調理して、ひと鉢に盛り合わせた、日本料理のサラダです。

Seasonal Salad

I've always had a desire to enhance the value of a vegetable dish served in traditional and formal Japanese restaurants. I wanted to express each character of the vegetable in a simple but impressive way, so I can serve an exquisite vegetable dish in my course meal. Salad is a dish I've been tackling ever since opening this restaurant. When I started out nine years ago, I remember that 50% of guests did not finish their salad. Especially Japanese men of the older generation. They just don't eat salad. They don't seem to like raw vegetables. So I wanted to create a dish, where the flavour of each vegetable is both distinctive and enjoyable. It was a search for "a Japanese cuisine salad".

The flavour of Japanese vegetables are not as strong as those of Europe and other Asian countries. So I've decided to explore the delicate flavour of Japanese vegetables, taking a different approach in cooking to best match the delicate characteristic of each vegetable. Do I simmer, boil, fry, or pickle? What is the best temperature for deep-frying this vegetable? I take intense care in preparing for even one leaf, one slice of an eggplant.

I usually use variations of about 20 vegetables a day. I'd carefully look over the vegetables each morning and decide what I wanted to do with them. Vegetables are delivered from my sister's farm in Chiba prefecture. Green vegetables and root vegetables grown at my sister's farm are a big support to me. I use soy oil for my vegetable dish, especially for the finishing touch, because it doesn't stand out strongly. Just a small portion of it is enough. I don't add vinegar, just a small amount of *shio-kombu* (salty *kombu*). Sometimes I'm asked if this is the Japanese version of Michelle Bras' Gargouille. No, this is similar to our traditional vegetable dish "*taki-awase*" (vegetables cooked individually, but served together in one bowl).

左上から／にこにこにんじん／ビーツの甘酢漬け／トマトの甘酢漬け／煮ごぼう／からすえんどう／きくいものチップ／茎ブロッコリの素揚げ／インカのめざめの素揚げ／のびる／ミニにんじんソテー／紫ケール素揚げ／三つ葉の若芽／芽きゃべつ素揚げ／きゃべつの新芽／ルーコラの花芽／食用花／食用つばき／サラダ菜類

pickled carrot / pickled beetroot / pickled tomato / simmered burdock / boiled vetch / Jerusalem artichoke chip / stick broccoli / deep-fried "Inka" potato / wild rocambole / sautéed mini carrot / violet kale / Japanese honeywort sprout / deep-fried Brussels sprout / cabagge sprout / garden roquet flower / edible flowers / edible camellia / lettuces

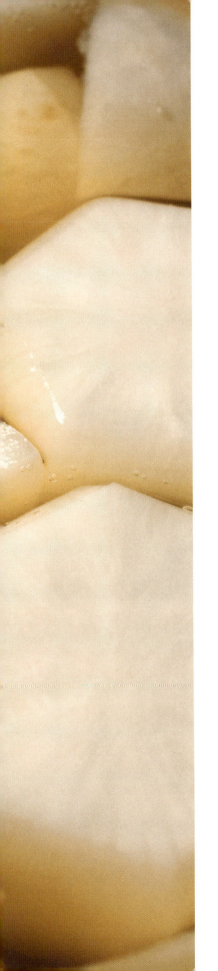

三、焼きもの、煮もの

3. Grilled and simmered

時鮭
万願寺とうがらし
赤葉玉ねぎ

「時知らず」とも呼ばれる初夏の鮭を、軽く干してから
焼きました。この時期ならではの繊細な旨みをしっか
りと味わえるよう、大ぶりのカットで。皮下の脂が少
ないので、油分を補う意味で、揚げた夏野菜をこれま
た大胆に添えます。

Tokisake salmon

manganji pepper, red spring onion

Lightly dry and grill early summer salmon. To thoroughly enjoy
the delicate umami of this season, cut the salmon into large pieces.
There's not much fat under the skin, to add richness serve it with
deep-fried summer vegetables.

夏のごちそう、鮎の塩焼き。丸ごとがぶりと食べたときの香ばしさ、爽やかな苦みは何とも言えないおいしさ。ですが、魚の頭や骨を食べることに抵抗がある方も少なくありません。そこで＜頭を落とした干物＋肝の塩辛パテ＋たで風味の蒸しパン＞に再構成しました。干物の塩は軽めなので、焼きたての身はふんわり。皮やヒレはしっかりと香ばしい。米粉でつくったたで蒸しパンはモチモチしてかすかに甘く、肝のパテによく合います。バゲットに肉パテをぬる感覚で楽しめます。

Grilled lightly-dried *ayu*, sweetfish

uruka pate, *tade* leaf steamed bread

Grilled *ayu* is a summer treat in Japan. To enjoy *ayu* sweetfish, grill it whole and eat it whole. When you bite into a whole fish, you'll taste the grilled flavour and refreshing bitterness. But, some people are not used to eating the fish head and bones. So I rearrange it like this, <lightly dried fish (without head) + *uruka,* ayu gut pate + steamed *tade* leaf flavoured rice bread>. *Tade* bread is sticky and bitter with a unique green note, a great combination with *uruka* pate. Enjoy it as if spreading meat pate on a baguette.

さんまの朴葉焼き

肝味噌ソース
にこにこ銀杏
クスクスと雑穀のトースト
おばけさつまいも

さんまは丸ごと塩焼きにするのが一番おいしい！と思うものの、外国の方にその魅力を伝えるには、少々の"翻訳"が必要です。食べやすく、わかりやすく、とくに肝の苦みをおいしいと感じてもらうにはどうすればいい？──それがこの料理のテーマ。身は、骨からはずし軽く干してから焼き、肝は味噌と混ぜて「ソース」にしました。たっぷりとかけたクスクスと雑穀はソースをじっくりと味わうための相棒。香ばしさが肝の旨みによく合います。

Grilled pacific saury on big leaf

liver *miso* sauce, roasted gingko nut,
cuscus and grain on toast, sweet potato chip

The best way to enjoy *sanma*, pacific saury is simply salt-grilling the whole fish, and eating the flesh with liver. I wanted to make an easy to eat *sanma* dish for foreign guests. I took out the bones and dried lightly, then roasted it with salt. For sauce, I mixed *miso* with liver. To savor liver sauce, serve it with a generous amount of cuscus and grain.

ヤキザカナの価値

The great Japanese "*yaki-zakana*"

西洋料理の世界では、いわゆる"低温調理"の流行が続いています。低温調理とは、たんぱく質が変性して分水が始まるぎりぎりの温度帯を維持しながらゆっくりと加熱することで、厚切り肉や厚切り魚の身を均一に、ジューシーに仕上げる、というものです。私が訪れたヨーロッパやアメリカのモダン系レストランの魚料理も皆これで、生温かめの、限りなくふわっとした仕上がりでした。

日本の焼き魚のコンセプトはある意味、それとは真逆です。日本の焼き魚はしっかりと「焼き切る」。火の力で「香ばしさ」と「旨み」をぐっと引き出すイメージでしょうか。強めの火でまず魚の脂を溶かし、水分が失われる前に焼き上げるのですが、大事なことは、焼く「前」にあります。目の前にある魚の脂の乗りを見きわめること。必要な量の塩をあて、必要な時間をおき、ときに干し、ときに熟成させること。そうして旨みを最大限に凝縮してから、一気に焼きます。

焼きの技術は塩の技術です。塩を使いこなすには感性が必要です。海外の最新モードを体験したことで、日本の伝統的な焼き魚が目指すところがより見えてきた気がします。

Low-temperature cooking is still a trend in occidental cuisine.

By slowly heating at a low temperature not to degenerate protein and diverse moisture, thick slices of meat and fish are uniformly cooked preserving the moist texture. The modern style high-end restaurants I have visited in Europe and America served fish cooked on a gentle low heat, it remained tender and succulent.

Yaki-zakana (Japanese-style grilled fish) takes the opposite approach. We use high heat to melt away the fish fat, and on medium-high heat quickly grill fish, the power of the flame bringing out the grilled aroma and umami. Technique is required in the process of getting the fish ready to grill. First, we must determine the amount of fat, and salt it sufficiently then let it rest for an adequate time. If necessary, dry or mature the fish. Using these steps, we condense and maximize umami, then the fish is ready to be grilled on a high heat.

He who learns to cook, must first learn to use salt. By experiencing the latest trend from overseas I'm able to see where I want to go with traditional Japanese *yaki-zakana*.

鰆の一夜干し

海苔酢
松茸のあぶり
すだち

脂ののった鰆を一夜干しに。皮下の脂をしっかりと、身はしっとりと
焼き上げて、焼き松茸の香りで包み込みます。魚にぬった海苔酢の酸
味と香りがアクセント。

Grilled Spanish mackerel

nori-vinegar sauce, grilled *matsutake*, *sudachi* citrus

Use fatty Spanish mackerel. Dry it overnight. Thoroughly cook the fat under the skin
and keep the flesh moist and tender. Arrange grilled *matsutake* on top, wrapping Spanish
mackerel with its aroma. Accent it with the acidity and fragrance of *nori*-vinegar sauce.

ブイヤベース

はも
あかざ海老
冬瓜

きりりとした旨みと、すっきりとした後味を目指した「和のブイヤ
ベース」。かつお節とトマトと玉ねぎでだしをとり、野菜の旨みと酸
味、魚の風味をバランスよくまとめています。トマトは昆布と同じグ
ルタミン酸が含まれているので、とくに海外での出仕事では昆布感覚
で使っています。

Bouillabaisse

hamo conger, langoustine, white gourd

The concept of this dish is "Japanese bouillabaisse": bouillabaisse with crisp umami and
a clean aftertaste. *Dashi* made from *katsuobushi*, tomato and onion has umami, acidity
and sweetness. This creates a great balance with seafood. Tomato has same glutamic
acid as *kombu*, so when working overseas, I use tomato in place of *kombu*.

甘鯛の揚げ焼き

焼き黒きゃべつ

甘鯛はうろこがおいしい魚です。皮を高温で揚げると、うろこが香ばしいチップスになり、それが外国の方にはユニークに映るようです。香りのアクセントとして添えたのが、黒きゃべつ。焼くと海藻のような香りになり、魚によく合うのです。口に入れるとホロホロッと溶けて香りだけが残るところも印象的。

Crispy scale tilefish
roasted black cabbage

Tilefish is a delicious fish, also known for its tasty scale. When deep-fried at a high temperature, the scale becomes like a crispy chip that appeals to foreign guests as a unique dish. I accent it with flavour of black cabbage. When grilled, black cabbage has the scent of seaweed, it goes well with fish. Cabbage melts away and leaves a distinctive aroma in your mouth.

えぼだいの一夜干し

根セロリのピュレ
まぐろ酒盗ソース
赤かぶチップ

えぼだいは開きにせず、食べやすいよう三枚におろし
てから干しています。焼いた身に、バターたっぷりの
根菜ピュレをのせ、塩気のきいた酒盗ソースをかけて
グラタン風に仕上げました。味わいの軽い魚なので、
旨み、香ばしさ、歯ごたえを「足し算」して構成した
お皿です。

Grilled butterfish
celeriac puree, tuna "*shuto*", red turnip chip

Fillet Butterfish and dry it overnight. Grill and top it with pureed
vegetable. Pour salty "*shuto* (salt fermented tuna gut)" sauce and
brown the surface like gratin. Because butterfish is a light flavoured
fish, I've added extra umami for richness, and crisp vegitable chips.

金華豚の煮焼き
水なすの素揚げ

金華豚は、脂身が甘くておいしい豚です。かつおだし
を煮含めてから、表面をあぶってロースト風に仕上げ、
焼いたとうもろこしの皮とハーブの上に盛りました。
夏らしい香ばしさが食欲を刺激します。

Stewed and roasted *Kinka* pork
Deep-fried eggplant

Kinka pork has a delicious fat with sweet flavour. Simmer pork in
katsuo-dashi, then sear the surface. Serve this on roasted corn skin
and herb. Wonderful summer aroma that stimulates the appetite.

サーロイン牛の
焼きしゃぶ
なすの焼き浸し
辛味大根おろし

表面だけさっとバーナーであぶったサーロイン牛の下
は、たっぷりの辛味大根おろしをのせた、焼きなすの
お浸し。だし＋醤油の少し濃い目の味がすべてをおい
しくまとめてくれます。夏感たっぷりの肉料理。

Beef sirloin *"yaki-shabu"*
grilled eggplant soaked in *dashi*, grated tangy *daikon*

Lightly sear sirloin beef with a culinary torch. Place the beef on top
of a generous amount of grated tangy *daikon* and grilled *katsuo-dashi*
soaked eggplant, *dashi* and the strong flavour of soy sauce binds the
ingredients together. A dish of meat to enjoy in summer time.

「日本料理の肉料理」

Japanese cuisine style meat dish

コースの中に1品は肉を使った料理を入れたいと思っています。

いろいろな料理を楽しんでも、最終的には肉を食べて満足感がおさまるというのが、とくに外国人には正直なところだと思います。これから日本料理が世界に出て、より多くの人に親しんでもらうには、肉という食材にもっと取り組んでいく必要があると感じます。

といっても、肉のおいしさで真っ向勝負しようとしたら焼き肉には勝てないし、おいしいソースを組み合わせたフレンチにも勝てません。そもそも日本料理店のキッチンには大きな肉の塊を調理できる機材がないですし、うちの店では規制上、炭火も使えません。

では、日本料理ならではの肉料理とは何なのでしょう。たとえば、味噌漬け的なもの。日本の発酵文化やマリネ文化が肉をおいしくしてくれます。もうひとつ、わたしが追いかけているテーマが「肉とかつおだしのハーモニー」です。肉の旨みに、かつおだしの旨みとスモーキー感、しっとり感が加わったときのおいしさは、日本料理だけのもの。肉をだしで煮るだけでなく、いったんゆでたり焼いたりした肉に、あらためてだしを煮含めることもあります。この「肉のお浸し」にはいろいろな味の段階や表現があり、とてもおもしろいと思っています。

肉料理は、煮ものや焼きものに限定せずに、ごはん料理とすることもあります。コース全体の流れや、お客さまのお腹具合をみながら、配分しています。

Within the course meal, I like to have at least one meat dish. Even after enjoying different types of dishes, it's probably the honest opinion of foreign guests that true satisfaction comes with a meat dish.

For further global recognition and familiarizing of Japanese cuisine, meat should take a greater role as an ingredient.

However, if we go head-on and serve it as "the meat dish", we can't compete with Korean barbecue or delicious combinations of French sauce and meat.

Japanese kitchens are usually not equipped for cooking large blocks of meat and unfortunately in our kitchen, we're unable to use *binchotan* charcoal due to fire regulations.

So how do we serve meat as Japanese cuisine? One example is traditional "*miso-zuke*", marinated in *miso*—umami fermentation makes the beef rich in flavour. I have also been pursuing the harmony of "meat and *katsuo-dashi*". Umami and slightly smoky scent of *katsuo-dashi* adds flavour and moist texture to meat. Not just simmering meat in *katsuo-dashi*, but soaking meat in *katsuo-dashi*, after boiling or roasting. This "meat *hitashi*" has different stages of flavour and different presentation styles, which I find very interesting.

Sometimes I'd serve it as a rice dish. I would observe, how guests are enjoying the course meal and how they're eating the dishes, then decide what to serve as a meat dish.

いのしし肩肉の
ロースト

血入り味噌ソース
根菜のチップス

日本のジビエ、いのししを低温でゆっくりとロースト
し、田楽味噌をベースにしたソースを合わせました。
土の中のものを食べるいのししは根菜との香りの相性
が抜群。「まず根菜のチップスを食べて口の中に土の香
りを感じてからお肉を食べてください」と申し添えます。

Roasted wild boar shoulder

miso "salmis" sauce, root vegetable chip

Wild boar meat, slowly roasted at a low temperature, serve with sauce
made with sweet *miso* and just a hint of wild boar blood. Wild boar
feeds on things inside the soil and its meat is compatible with aroma
of root vegetables. I recommend the guests to "first enjoy the aroma of
soil of vegetable chip, then the meat…"

かぶだし

かつお節
かぶの皮

新潟の酒、麒麟山の仕込み水を沸かし、かつお節をたっぷり加えます。味が出たところで、厚めにむいたかぶの皮を投入。味が出るまで20分間ほどコトコト煮たら火からおろし、そのまま置いて冷まします。完全に冷めてから静かに布ごしします。

Turnip-*dashi*
katsuobushi, turnip skin

Boil water (spring water used to brew *sake* "Kirin mountain" in Nigatta prefecture) and add *katsuobushi*. When the flavour of *katsuobushi* is extracted, add thickly peeled turnip skin. Simmer for about 10 minutes, remove from the heat and let it rest. When it has cooled, gently strain with cloth.

昆布ではなく
野菜と、
かつお節

No *kombu*, just *katsuobushi* and vegetable

傳では昆布をほとんど使いません。

献立に「一番だしのお椀」はないので、いわゆる一番だし（かつお節と昆布でとる、吸物用のだし）を取りません。そして煮もの全般に使う基本のだしにも、昆布は使わない。基本的にすべてのベースは、かつおだしです。

かつおだしの香りのはなやかさ、口に含んだ瞬間に脳に伝わるシャープな旨みが好き。だし初心者の外国人にもわかりやすいおいしさだと思います。ただ、かつおだしばかりだと、旨みがキレすぎて疲れる場面もあります。といって昆布を使うと旨みが重くなる。そこで昆布がわりに使っているのが「野菜だし」です。

これは、いわゆる精進だしではなく「かつお節＋野菜」でとるだしです（実際には、かつおだしで野菜を煮出すことが多いのですが）。野菜の甘みでかつおだしの旨みのカドがとれ、全体としては軽やかな風味にまとまります。

たとえば、冬はかぶ。かぶとかつお節でとるこの「かぶだし」で、たとえば金目鯛を炊くと、軽い甘さが魚の風味を引き立ててとてもおいしい。鴨鍋のベースにも使います。同様に、春にはたけのこの皮、夏はとうもろこし…、といろいろな野菜が使えます。とくに気に入っているのはもやしだしで、貝の三杯酢にとても合い、煮物の地や味噌汁としてもおいしく使えます。

野菜を使えばだしにも季節感が生まれます。その風味はバランス第一ですが、あえて野菜の甘みや香りを強く出したい場合は、追いがつおならぬ「追い野菜」で強化することも可能です。

At DEN, we rarely use *kombu*.

Many Japanese restaurants prepare *dashi* with *katsuobushi* and *kombu* to balance the flavour.

We basically use *katsuo-dashi* (*dashi* broth extracted from *katsuobushi*) for all our dishes.

Katsuo-dashi has a gorgeous aroma and clear umami that stimulates our brain when we take that first sip. Flavour, which is easy to understand for everyone, even for foreign guests trying it for the first time. For some dishes, *katsuo-dashi* can be too sharp. However, *kombu-dashi* can be too heavy. So we use "vegetable *dashi*". This is not a vegetarian *dashi*, its *dashi* of "*katsuobushi* & vegetables" (we often simmer vegetables in *katsuo-dashi*). Sweetness of the vegetable takes the edge off *katsuo-dashi* umami, making it light in flavour.

For example, in winter, red snapper simmered in "turnip *dashi*", dashi made from *katsuobushi* and turnip skin. This light and sweet *dashi*, highlights the flavour of the fish. We also use this *dashi* for duck hot pot. In spring "skin of bamboo shoot *dashi*", in summer "corn *dashi*". We can make *dashi* from many types of vegetables. My favorite is "bean sprout *dashi*", it goes well with shellfish sashimi and *sanbai*-vinegar-sauce, stewed dish, or *miso* soup.

With vegetable *dashi*, the sense of the season is present. Balancing the flavour is important, when you want to emphasize the sweetness and aroma of the vegetable, add extra vegetable in a way you would add extra *katsuobushi*.

鴨葱の
ブイヨン仕立て
かぶだし

鴨鍋風の煮ものです。ベースは、かつお節とかぶの皮
でとった「かぶだし」。鴨には甘みが合いますが、みり
んなどは使いません。だしの自然な甘さが、鴨の旨み
によくなじみます。

"Duck scallion" buillon
turnip *dashi*

Hot pot style, duck consomme. Basic broth is "turnip *dashi*" made
with *katsuobushi* and skin of turnip. Although sweet seasoning goes
well with duck, we don't use seasoning like *mirin* for this dish. The
natural sweetness of *dashi* blends in well with the duck's umami.

かぶと香箱がに

かぶは下ゆでをせず、直接かぶだしで炊き始めます。だしには追いかぶもして、かぶの風味をしっかりと強調。その甘みが、香箱がにのデリケートな旨みと好対照になります。

Turnip and *kobako*-crab

Don't pre-boil the turnip, simmer in "turnip *dashi*" and add extra turnip skin to highlight the flavour. The sweetness of turnip makes a good contrast to the delicate umami of *kobako*-crab.

根菜のくず餡

野菜料理には日本料理の根っこのようなものがあると
思います。修業時代、師匠である親父さんがつくるお
でんの大根が大好きでした。滋味があってほっとする、
日常の野菜料理をきわめたい…そんな気分でつくって
いる煮ものです。

Root vegetable with "*kudzu an*" sauce

For me, the vegetable dish is "the root" of Japanese cuisine. I love
"*oden*" (winter hot pot) especially *daikon*-radish cooked by my
mentor. It's a wholesome and heartwarming everyday vegetable dish.
That is what I'd like to excel at. This is what goes through my mind
as I'm cooking this dish.

牛ほほ肉の
薬膳うしお仕立て

牛ほほ肉をいったんゆで、さらにかつおだしで煮込んで、だしを煮含めています。このときの煮汁＝スープが、この料理の主役。たっぷりの新玉ねぎと薬膳材料を加えて仕上げました。しょうがをきかせたさっぱりの塩味。身体にやさしい夏のアツアツ料理です。

"Yakuzen ushio" style beef cheek

A dish of beef cheek simmered in *katuo-dashi*. For a finishing touch, add a generous amount of seasonal onion and sweet spices of *"yakuzen"*, oriental medical cuisine. The soup, an extract of all ingredients is the soul of the dish, with simple salt seasoning and ginger flavour. A piping-hot summer dish, good for your health.

豚肩ロースと
すぐきの椀

かつおだしに豚肉とすぐき菜の旨みをプラス。乳酸発
酵の青菜に特有な酸味とコクが加わって、スープの味
わいがより深くなります。酸っぱさが食欲を刺激して、
よく煮込まれた大きな豚肉もすっきりとお腹に。

Pork shoulder loin & *suguki* soup

Suguki-na, lactic fermented green vegetable, have unique acidity
which enriches the flavor of the soup. Sourness stimulates the
appetite. Simmered chunks of pork are kind to digestion.

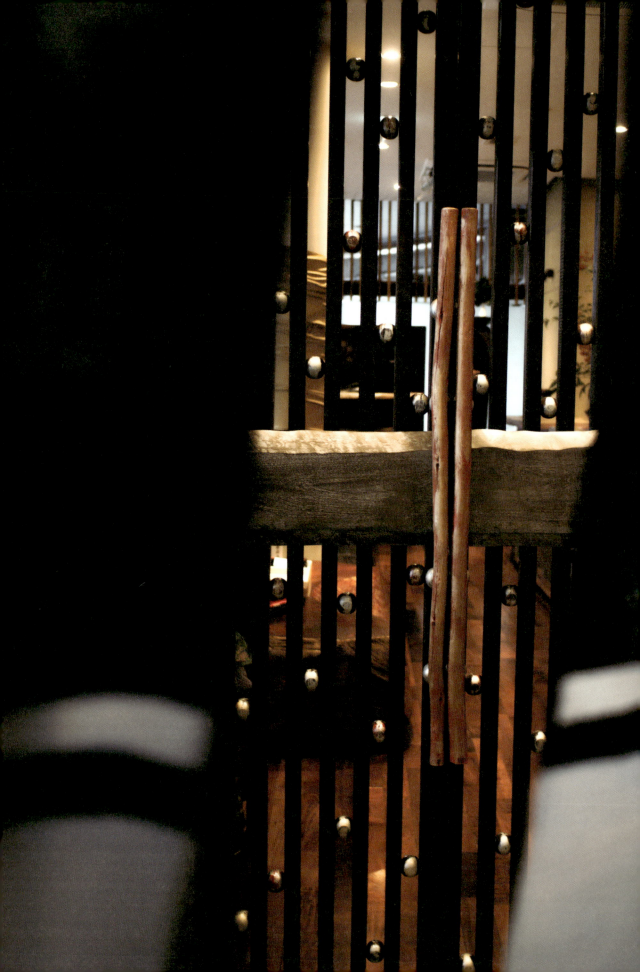

四、ごはんとデザート

4. Rice and dessert

ごはんはメインディッシュ

Rice dish as a main dish

「日本料理を表現する」という視点にたつと、ごはんはとても魅力的な分野です。

これまで高級日本料理のコースメニューにおいては、「ごはん」は食事のクライマックスの「後」にありました。たくさんのご馳走をお酒と一緒に楽しんだ後ですから、締めは白ごはんとお漬物でシンプルに。あるいは少し工夫して、季節の炊き込みごはん、といったところでしょう。

でも、外国の方にとっては「日本＝米」、ごはん料理こそ日本料理です。むしろ、ごはん料理をクライマックスとしてもよいのかもしれない。少なくとも、ごはん料理にもわくわく感やご馳走感を表現したほうが、確実にポイントが高いように思います。

日本のごはんと肉、ごはんと魚、ごはんと野菜とのコンビネーションから生まれるおいしさは、肉や魚単体のおいしさとは別ものです。私たちが日常の食事で楽しんでいるそのおいしさこそが、大きな感動につながります。

ごはんとひとことに言ってもいろいろな調理や食べ方があります。季節感も出しやすく、量も調整しやすい。満腹感のあるメインディッシュにもなれば、プリモピアット風にも、もちろんシンプルな締めの一品にもなります。つくる側としても、可能性がたくさんあって楽しいのです。日本のごはんのおいしさを、料理店のスタイルに落とし込むおもしろさがあります。

When I think about how I would express "Japanese cuisine", rice is an interesting and attractive ingredient to pursue.

At *ryotei*, a traditional and formal Japanese restaurant, the rice dish comes after the high point of a course meal. We would end the meal with simple white rice with pickles or be a little more creative and cook rice with seasonal ingredients.

But I think "rice dish" symbolizes Japanese cuisine for foreign guests. With this in mind, rice can be "the dish" served at a high point of a course meal. At least, rice dishes should be exciting and special.

Japanese combination of "rice with meat", "rice with fish", "rice with vegetable", bring out special flavours. It's different from eating meat or fish as a single ingredient. Deliciousness that makes a great impression.

There are many ways to cook and eat rice. It partners well with seasonal ingredients and the quantity is easily adjustable. It can be served as a seasonal dish, fulfilling main dish or primo piatto and of course as simple final dish of a course meal. Rice has a lot of possibilities and it's a fun ingredient to prepare with.

みすじごはん

おろしわさび

牛肉の塊の表面を焼き固め、だしで煮て、そのあと一週間、追いがつおをしただしに浸しておきます。いうならば「肉のお浸し」。ごはんの上にどんとのった姿はいかにも「肉の塊」ですが、いざ食べるとやわらかい。すっと噛み切れて、熟成肉のような練れた香りが口に広がります。肉を土鍋のごはんにのせた状態でプレゼンテーションしてから、切り分けます。

Beef top-blade rice

grated *wasabi*

Sear the block of meat, simmer in *katsuo-dashi*, then add extra *katsuobushi* and rest it for a week. "Lump of meat" on rice may seem overwhelming, but it's tender and easy to bite into. It has a refined flavour of matured meat.

富士山麓
きのこごはん

スタッフ全員参加のきのこ狩りは恒例行事の楽しい遠足ですが、帰ったら即、仕事が待っています。天然きのこは時間勝負。すぐに掃除して全種まとめてオイル漬けして、香りを封じ込めます。食べるときに強火でソテーすれば香ばしさが生き返る。歯ごたえいろいろ、秋の風味が詰まった混ぜごはんです。

Mt.Fuji mushroom rice

All staff of my restaurant attend and enjoy the annual mushroom hunting. But as soon as we return, work awaits us. With wild mushroom, time is of the essence. Quickly clean and confit it in oil to preserve the aroma. When serving, saute in high heat to bring back the aroma. A rice dish to enjoy the texture and aroma of autumn mushrooms.

いくらごはん

生いくらを、醤油入りのだしで「お浸し」にしました。
一般的な醤油漬けでは味わえない、まさにザ・卵の風
味。口の中でぷちんとはじけたときのジューシー感が
とくに印象的です。

Salmon roe rice

Soak raw salmon roe in soy seasoned *dashi*. This "*hitashi*" soaking
brings out the natural flavour of roe, different from the usual soy
sauce marinate. Enjoy the distinctive sensation of juicy roe popping
in your mouth.

サーロインごはん

牛サーロインの生スライスを炊きたてごはんにのせて、サラマンダーで火入れ。杓文字で肉を切りながらごはんとよく混ぜ、脂の旨みを全体になじませてお茶碗によそいます。大事なポイントはごはんにおこげをつくっておくこと。カリカリの香ばしさがアクセントになって、食べ飽きせずについついごはんが進みます。

Beef sirloin rice

Place slices of raw beef sirloin on freshly cooked rice in an earthenware pot. Heat it in a salamander. When mixing with rice, use a spatula to cut meat and thoroughly mix in the flavour of beef fat. Serve in a rice bowl. Make sure there are some scorched rice. Crispiness will be an accent to the flavour, and will stimulate the appetite.

かきごはん

かきは炊き込まずに、バターと醤油で炒めたものを、
その焼き汁ごと土鍋で炊いた白ごはんにのせています。
バター醤油でコーティングしたかきは、オイスターソー
スのような香りとコクで、白いごはんによく合うこと！
カキをつぶしながらごはんとしっかり混ぜ合わせてか
ら、お茶碗によそいます。

Oyster rice

Saute oyster with butter and soy sauce, then place it on top of white
rice. Oyster coated with butter and soy sauce has impact which makes
it a delicious contrast with the plain white rice. Mix oyster and rice
well, serve in a rice bowl.

ほんのりではなく、はっきり

Not soft and subtle but strong and clear flavour

ごはんはお客さまごとに土鍋で炊いています。日本人の常連さんのなかには締めは必ず白ごはんで、という方もいらっしゃいますが、外国の方は基本的に、味付きごはんがお好みです。といっても、炊き込みごはんはあまりつくりません。このかきごはんも、炊き込みごはんではなく「混ぜごはん」です。

個人的には炊き込みごはんが大好きです。うすく味をつけただしでごはんと旬の具材を炊きこんで、仕上げに柚子と三つ葉でものせれば、大満足。淡い味のハーモニーがごはんの香りを引き立て、旬のたけのこや旬のかきの風味をしみじみと引き立ててくれます。

でもこれ、海外ではあまり受けません。たいていは「味がない、うすい」と言われます。「ごはんと具の淡い味のハーモニー」は、世界のだれにでも共感してもらえるわけではないようです。"かきの料理なのに、肝心のかきの味がぼんやりしている"ことがピンとこない、という感じでしょうか。

主役素材がそれ単体でおいしいとわかることが重要なのだと思います。「ほんわかした」、「えもいわれぬ」、「微妙な」ではなく、かきがおいしいと一発でわかることが大切です。パーツパーツがおいしく、そして、トータルでもおいしいこと。

旬のおいしさをより多くの人に感じていただくために留意している構成ポイントです。

Rice is cooked in an earthenware pot for each party of guests. Some Japanese guests would only order simple white rice. But foreign guests basically prefer seasoned rice.

But, I rarely cook seasoned "takikomi-gohan" (rice cooked with ingredients), our oyster rice is "maze-gohan" (rice and ingredients cooked separately then mixed).

Personally, I like "takikomi-gohan", rice and ingredients cooked with lightly flavored *dashi*, such as rice with bamboo shoots or oyster. As a finishing touch, I like to sprinkle *yuzu* zest and *mitsuba* (wild chervil) on top. This harmony of delicate flavour brings out the natural taste of rice and ingredients.

However, this combination is not popular overseas. We've received comments like "flavour is too weak".

I understand that it's importance for the main ingredient to stand out as an individual ingredient. Not "gentle" "indescribable" "subtle", but to be able to taste the impact of oyster in the first mouthful. And it's also important for the whole meal to be satisfying. To prepare seasonal ingredients in a way so that guests can appreciate its flavour. I believe these are important factors to consider when creating a menu.

ポルチーニごはん

イタリアで、友人シェフが乾燥ポルチーニの生産者を紹介してくれました。大きくて肉厚。旨みが濃いのはもちろん、香りにまったく濁りがありません。これをもどして松茸ごはん風の炊き込みごはんにします。複雑な秋の香りも、むっちりした歯ごたえも、ふっくら炊き上がったごはんによく合い、ちゃんと日本料理になっています。もどし汁で炊きますが、そのままでは香りが濃すぎるのでかつおだしで割り、やや醤油をきかせてバランスをとります。

Porcini rice

My friend in Italy introduced me to a renowned producer of dried porcini. Large and thick porcinis with rich umami and clear aroma. Rehydrate porcini and prepare it like *matsutake* rice. Cook rice with porcini juice and *katsuo-dashi* to make it mild. Balance the flavour with soy sauce. Enjoy the texture and the autumn aroma.

白子の雑炊

黒こしょう

白ごはんをだしでやわらかく煮て、火を止めてから白子を加えて混ぜ込みます。リゾットにパルメザンチーズを加えてつなぐような感じです。クリーミーで、季節の旨み濃厚。これでまだお酒がいけます。

Milt of cod *zosui*

black pepper

Simmer white rice in *katsuo-dashi*, until it's soft. Turn off the heat and add milt of cod, stir gently as though adding parmesan cheese to risotto. This "zosui" risotto is creamy and rich with seasonal flavour. You'd want another glass of *sake*.

ほほ肉ごはん

ふっくらと煮上げた牛ほほ肉を、こまかく割いてだし
ごはんの上に。どっしりとしたメイン的なごはん料理
ではなく、料理をひと通り召し上がって「最後に何か
もう少し」「軽くごはんを」といったシチュエーション
でお出ししています。

Beef cheek rice

Shredded tender simmered beef cheek on a small bowl of *dashi* rice —
this is not a type of main dish, but as "something light at the end of
meal".

からすみ雑炊

炊いたごはんをかつおだしで軽く煮て、リゾット風に
仕上げています。具はなし。味付けも軽めにして、あ
ぶったからすみをたっぷりとのせます。

Bottarga *zosui*

Lightly simmer cooked rice in *katsuo-dashi*, adding no other ingredient.
Lightly season and top it generously with bottarga.

宝石ごはん

しみじみとしたおいしさの、根菜の炊き込みごはん。土鍋の蓋を開けたときにふわっと立ち上る香りと、目に飛び込む彩りが醍醐味です。根菜はそのときどきで、色合いのバランスを考えて選びます。にんじんばかり5種類を使って「うさぎごはん」とすることも。

Jewelry rice

Savour the gentle flavour of root vegetables with rice. Open the lid of an earthenware pot and enjoy the aroma and the bright colours. Choose seasonal root vegetables with a colour combination in mind. I sometimes prepare "bunny rice", using five different colours of carrots.

あくまでも、水菓子

"water sweets"

日本のかつての料亭では、食後は「水菓子」と称してくだものを出すのが定石でした。昔は、おいしいくだもの自体がぜいたく品です。ただのくだものといえばそれまでですが、芸術品のような姿、香り、味のものを選び、ベストに熟した状態を和包丁でシャープにカットしておいしい旬を伝える…これもたしかに、日本料理だと思います。

傳のデザートも、水菓子です。

正確にいうなら、水菓子の進化版です。旬のくだもののおいしさを、新しい印象で伝えたいと思っています。びわの香りを引き立てるものは？ 柿と相性のよい甘さは？ 桃の舌触りを強調するには？…といったところから発想は始まり、ときには大胆に、くだものの個性を飛躍させる素材を取り合わせます。

具体的な構成は、葛切りや水羊羹のような日本のスイーツを題材にしたり、あるいはフレンチやイタリアンの創作デザート風に組み立ててから、和食寄りの香りを配すこともあります。海外の研修生が提案してくれたアイディアから、素材の意外な相性に気づかされることもあります。

もうひとつ、とくに大切にしているのがワクワク感です。レストランの創作デザートのような華やかさがあり、しかも日本料理らしくシンプルで、清潔感のあるものを。それが目に入ったら最後にまたテンションがあがるような、「食後のお愉しみ」です。

At *ryotei*, a traditional and formal Japanese restaurant, it was standard to serve fruit as "*mizu-gashi*" ("water sweets") for dessert. In the olden days, delicious fruits were considered a luxury item. Fruit with artistic shape, aroma and flavour were carefully chosen, and when perfectly ripe, cut into a shape using a sharp Japanese knife. One of the Japanese cuisine style of expressing seasonal delight.

DEN's dessert is "*mizu-gashi*".

To be accurate, it's a modern and improved version of *mizu-gashi*. I wanted to give a new impression to the delicious flavour of seasonal fruits. What brings out the aroma of loquat? What goes well with sweetness of *kaki*? How can I accentuate the texture of peach? I started out with these questions, and sometimes I'd be bold in the combination to find new ways to enjoy the fruit.

Actual ideas may originate from Japanese sweets such as "*kudzu-kiri*"(*kudzu* starch noodles) and "*mizu-yokan*" (sweet bean jelly). Or we can be creative like French or Italian desserts, and add Japanese flavour to it. Ideas of trainee from abroad can sometimes make me realize the unexpected match of ingredients.

And of course, that feeling of excitement and expectation is important. It should be as glamourous as modern cuisine, simple and clean as Japanese cuisine. For me, dessert is "a special surprise at the end of a meal".

梨のワンショット

カモミールティー

香りとのど越しを楽しむ、甘み控えめのドリンク。お口代わりのプレデザートですが、デザートはいらない、というお客さまにもおすすめできるワンショットです。

Chamomile flavoured Asian pear soup

A drink to enjoy the aroma and the smoothness. Lightly sweetened "single shot drink". Recommend as a refreshing pre-dessert for guests not interested in ordering dessert.

ハイビスカスの
グラニテ

カシスと紫芽のムース

ハイビスカスティーと発泡性ワインでつくったグラ
ニテに、赤じそ風味のふわふわムースをのせたフ
ローズンドリンクです。ムースのベースはカシスの
ピュレ。

Hibiscus granite

cassis and red *shiso* sprout mousse

This is granite made with hibiscus tea and sparkling wine—a
frozen drink topped with red *shiso* sprout flavoured fluffy mousse.
The basic ingredient for the mousse is cassis puree.

梨のピンチョス

この店で1年間研修したフランス人のパティシエが
います。日本の水菓子のコンセプトを説明したら、
彼なりの解釈で、水菓子風の手を加えすぎないくだ
もののデザートを提案してくれました。このプレデ
ザートも、そのひとつです。

Asian pear pincho

I explained the concept of "*mizu-gashi*" to a French patissier
training at our restaurant. He interpreted "*mizu-gashi*" in his way,
and suggested this pre-dessert.

夏の白雪

白桃
ココナッツのブランマンジェ
ヨーグルトかき氷
クリームチーズのソース

フレッシュの白桃、ブランマンジェ、カキ氷…テクス
チャーの異なる「白」の組み合わせです。スプーンで
すくうたびに、味わいがいろいろに変化します。

Summer snow

white peach, coconut blanc-manger,
yogurt shaved ice, cream cheese sauce

Fresh white peach, blanc-manger and shaved ice, a combination of
different textures and a combination of white ingredients. Variety of
flavour to be enjoyed in each spoonful.

はっか風味の
水羊羹
スパイスシロップ

はっかのハーブティーと漉し餡を合わせて、水羊羹をつくりました。はっかの香りは小豆の風味をぐっと引き立ててくれます。アフターノートがすっきりして、水羊羹の涼感もいっそう冴えます。

Japanese mint flavoured red bean jelly
spicy syrup

Mix, Japanese mint herb tea with strained red bean paste to make red bean jelly. Scent of Japanese mint enhances the red bean flavour. The aftertaste is refreshingly cool.

黒いちじくと
フォワグラクリーム

フォワグラの味噌漬けにホイップクリームを合わせた
ムースを、よく熟した黒いちじくと重ねました。ひと
つひとつは極小ポーション。食後酒に合わせる小さな
デザートです。

Black fig and foie gras cream

Mousse made with *miso* marinated foie gras and whipped cream. Top
it with ripe black fig. As a small dessert to enjoy with digestif.

ルバーブのコンポート

スイカ
ラムゼリーとアマレットゼリー
花穂じそ
紫芽

ルバーブが大好きです。ルバーブの酸味はちょっと梅に通じるものを感じるので、海外の出仕事では梅肉がわりによくルバーブを使います。そしておもしろいことに、ルバーブにも赤紫蘇がよく合います（赤じそ入りのルバーブジャムを鱧に合わせると、おいしい）。ルバーブ＋赤じその相性を軸にしたデザートです。

Rhubarb compote
watermelon, rum jelly and amaretto jelly,
shiso blossom, red *shiso* sprout

I love rhubarb. It has acidity similar to *ume*, Japanese plum—when working overseas, I use rhubarb in place of ume. *Ume* goes well with red *shiso* and I found that rhubarb is compatible with red *shiso*. This dessert is based on a great combination of rhubarb and red *shiso*.

秋のくだもの、
コワントロー風味
ヨーグルトシャーベット

フルーツにオレンジブランデーを合わせるという王道
の組み合わせを、日本料理風にアレンジしました。か
すかに温かいくず餡はコワントローの香り。フルーツ
をやさしく包みます。

Autumn fruit wrapped
in Cointreau flavour
yogurt sherbet

A combination of fruit and orange brandy, arranged in a Japanese
dessert style. Place a variety of fruits cut into bite-size pieces in a
bowl. Gently wrap fruit with slightly warm *kudzu* sauce scented with
Cointreau.

柿のコンポートと
クリームチーズの
ムース
黒蜜ソース
ラム酒のゼリー

柿にはラムが合います。ここでは柿をコンポートにし
ていますが、熟した柿をそのまま使うことも。

Kaki compote with cream cheese mousse
black sugar syrup, rum jelly

Kaki goes well with rum. *Kaki* compote is used here, but with ripe
kaki, use it as it is.

凍りいちじく、
味噌ベシャメルがけ

凍ったいちじくに、ぽてっとした舌触りの熱いソース
をかけました。プチプチしたいちじくの歯ごたえとと
味噌が焦げた香りがアクセントになります。

Frozen fig, with *miso* béchamel

A plump frozen fig with warm sauce with pudgy thickness. Fig's popping
texture and scent of scorched *miso* give an accent to this dessert.

ビーツと赤ワインの
レデュクション

ミルクアイス
カシス
花穂じそ
紫芽

海外からの研修生は、日本の素材から思わぬ個性を見
つけてくれます。フランス人のパティシエがとくに気
に入っていたのが、赤じそとカシスとの相性。たしか
に合わせて使うと香りがいっそうきわ立ちます。いろ
いろなデザートが生まれました。

Beetroot and red wine reduction
milk ice cream, cassis, *shiso* blossom, red *shiso* sprout

Trainees from abroad sometimes discover unexpected characteristics
in Japanese ingredients. A French patissier was very much taken
by the compatibility of Japanese *shiso* and cassis. Finding this
combination of aroma led to creating various new desserts.

傳のおせち料理

ふだんは日本料理の現代化に取り組んでいますが、お
せち料理だけは例外です。献立内容は伝統そのもの。
おせち料理は一品一品に意味があり、何日も前から乾
物をもどすなど、こつこつと仕事を重ねる過程に日本
料理の原点が詰まっています。年に一度、おせちの仕
事を通して日本料理をふり返りたい、若いスタッフに
伝えたいと思っています。

DEN's Osechi-Ryori

DEN is associated with "modern Japanese cuisine" the only exception
being *osechi-ryori* (traditional Japanese New Year's dishes assorted
in special boxes). DEN's osechi menu is completely traditional.
Each dish is an expression of praying for happiness. The process of
preparing seasonal *osechi*-food — reconstituting dry food over several
days, simmering for a long time etc. follows the extensive traditional
Japanese cooking rules and techniques.

料理解説

Recipes

基本のだし、合わせ調味料など

[かつおだし（基本）]
　かつお節[※1]　800g
　水（新潟の酒「麒麟山」の仕込み水）　5L
鍋に水を入れて火にかける。沸騰したら火を止め、かつお節を入れる。かつお節がすっかり沈んだら漉す。[※2]

※1　かつお節は荒節と枯節を混ぜて使用。時期によってその比率、血合いの有無、削りの厚さを調整している。
※2　必要に応じて追いがつおをして旨みを強めたり、野菜と一緒に煮出して「野菜だし」にしたりと、使い分けてる。

[土佐醤油]
　こいくち醤油　1.8L
　酒　360ml
　昆布　約20cm
　かつお節（追いがつお用）　1つかみ
こいくち醤油、酒、昆布を鍋に合わせて火にかける。沸いたら火を止め、追いがつおをする。そのまま丸1日置き、漉す。

[めんつゆ]
　かつおだし　720ml
　こいくち醤油　90ml
　みりん　90ml
　かつお節（追いがつお用）　1つかみ
　しょうがの搾り汁　適量
かつおだし、こいくち醤油、みりんを合わせて火にかける。沸騰したら火を止め、追いがつおをする。冷まして漉す。（好みで）適量のしょうがの搾り汁を加える。

[甘酢]
　水　200ml
　穀物酢　200ml
　砂糖　90g
材料を混ぜ合わせる。

[土佐酢]
　米酢　360ml
　かつおだし　180ml
　砂糖　60g
　みりん　180ml
　うすくち醤油　180ml
　かつお節（追いがつお用）　3〜4つかみ

材料（追いがつお用のかつお節以外）を鍋に合わせて火にかける。沸騰したら火を止め、追いがつおをする。そのまま丸1日置き、漉す。

[天ぷら衣]
小麦粉とコーンスターチを2対1の割合で合わせ、適量のビールで溶く。

[玉味噌]
　白こし味噌　2kg
　卵黄　15個
　砂糖　360g
　みりん　180ml
　酒　180ml
材料を鍋に合わせ、中火にかけて練り上げる。

[田楽味噌]
　赤味噌　2kg
　卵黄　15個
　砂糖　1kg
　酒　570ml
　みりん　570ml
材料を鍋に合わせ、中火にかけて練り上げる。

料理解説の表記について
・以下の頁では傳の料理を知っていただくために、つくり方の概略を説明しています。
・記載されている材料の分量や調理時間は、おおよその目安です。
・分量配合表に「何人分」等の表記がないものは、営業用の仕込み量、またはつくりやすい量の参考例です。
・材料、分量表記についての注釈
　昆布（だし用には基本的に日高昆布を使用）
　砂糖（上白糖を使用）
　フルール・ド・セル（ゲランド産のフレークソルト）
　1合＝180ml
　1L＝1リットル

一〇ページ

トマトのところてん

じゅんさい　パッションフルーツの種
バジルシード　土佐酢ゼリー

［トマトのところてん］
　　トマト　大6個
　　水　3L
　　てんぐさ　約60g（ひと晩水に浸けてもどす）
　　トマトジュース　300ml
トマトのざく切り、てんぐさ、水を鍋に合わせ、火
にかける。てんぐさが溶けたら火を止め、トマト
ジュースを加えて漉す。
流し缶に流し、冷蔵庫で冷やし固める。提供時に、
ところ天突きで突く。

［土佐酢ゼリー］
　　土佐酢（一一三ページ参照）　540ml
　　ゼラチン　10g（水でもどす）
土佐酢にゼラチンを加えて煮溶かす。流し缶に流し、
冷蔵庫で冷やし固める。

［トマトのマリネ酢］
　　トマト　適宜
　　米酢　200ml
　　水　200ml
　　砂糖　90g
材料を合わせて、トマトを漬け込む（トマトはサラ
ダに使う）。

［仕上げ］
トマトのところ天を器に盛る。じゅんさい、パッショ
ンフルーツの種、バジルシードをあしらい、スプー
ンで軽くくずした土佐酢ゼリーをのせる。
器にはすの葉をかぶせ、トマトのマリネ酢を少量落
とす。

一二ページ

ビーツの穴子挟み揚げ、
しそ風味

あなごを三枚におろし、身を3〜4cm幅に切る。
大きめのビーツを極薄の輪切りにする。
あなごを大葉で挟み、2枚の薄切りビーツ（あなご
の幅に合わせて適宜切る）で挟む。二等分して小麦
粉をまぶし、うすめに仕立てた天ぷら衣（一一三ペー
ジ）にくぐらせ、揚げる。

一三ページ

はもかつ

塩すだち

1kg以上のはもをおろし、半身にして骨切りする。4
〜5cm幅に切る。小麦粉をまぶし、卵液にくぐらせ、
パン粉をつけて白絞油で揚げる。
器に盛り、塩すだち（すだちの薄切りを粗塩で軽く
もんだもの）を4〜5枚添える。フルール・ド・セ
ルをふりかける。

一四ページ

ミニうに丼

おろしわさび　海ぶどう

ひとりにつき、むらさきうに2個を使用。

殻からうにの身をはずす。そのうち半量は、こいくち醤油、酒、みりんを1対1対1で合わせて煮切った地に約10分間漬ける。残り半量は生のまま使う。少しかために炊いたごはんに、とびこを混ぜる。うにの殻の中に盛り、生うにをのせる。その上に、うにの漬けを重ねて盛る。おろしわさびを盛り、海ぶどうを添える。

一五ページ
山いもの昆布締め
たたきおくら　温泉卵

やまいもをかつらむきし、極細のせん切りにする。バットに昆布を敷いてやまいもを並べ、さらに昆布を重ねる。半日置く。

おくらを刃叩きしてなめらかな餡にする。やまいもを器に盛り、温泉卵をのせる。めんつゆ（一一三ページ）をかけ、おくら餡とおくらの花を添える。

一六ページ
うにと生ゆばのべっこう餡
おろしわさび

［べっこう餡　10～12人分］
　かつおだし　360ml
　こいくち醤油　20ml
　みりん　20ml
　砂糖　約15g
　葛粉（水で溶く）　適量
かつおだしを火にかける。こいくち醤油、みりん、砂糖でやや甘めに味つけし、葛引きして火を止める。

［仕上げ］
器に生ゆばを盛り、生うにをのせる。べっこう餡をたっぷりとかける。おろしたてのわさびを天に盛る。

一七ページ
穴子の天ぷらとなすのお浸し
おくら餡　ぶぶあられ

あなごを三枚におろす。小麦粉をまぶし、天ぷら衣にくぐらせて、揚げる。

なすを網で焼き、皮をむく。味つけしただし（かつおだし12、こいくち醤油0.5、みりん0.5の比率）に浸しておく。

おくらを刃叩きしてなめらかな餡にする。べっこう餡（「うにと生ゆばのべっこう餡」参照）をつくり、火を止めて温度が落ち着いたところで、おくらを合わせる。

器になすのお浸しを盛り、あなごをのせる。おくら餡をこんもりとのせ、ぶぶあられを散らす。

一八ページ
きのこ豆腐
粟麩　赤こんにゃく　揚げぎんなん　ぶぶあられ

［きのこ豆腐］
　天然きのこ　500g
　かつおだし　適量
　牛乳　1280ml
　葛粉　180g
富士山麓で摘んだ数種の自生きのこ（やまいぐち、はないぐち、ぼりぼり、やまどりたけもどき、あみたけなど）を掃除する。かつおだしでさっとゆで、引き上げる。これをミキサーにかけ（必要ならだし

を少量足す）、すり流し状にする。
葛粉と牛乳を合わせ、ダマがなくなるまで混ぜる。すり流しを加え、混ぜて生地を均一にする。鍋にとって弱火にかけ、（ごま豆腐の要領で）しゃもじで練りながらゆっくりと火を入れる。流し缶に流し、冷蔵庫で冷やし固める。

[仕上げ]
きのこ豆腐を正方形に切る。片栗粉をまぶして、揚げる。粟麸とぎんなんをそれぞれ素揚げする。
赤こんにゃくをきのこ形に抜き、味つけしただし（かつおだし12、こいくち醤油0.5、みりん0.5の比率）で煮る。
椀にきのこ豆腐、粟麸、こんにゃくを盛り、揚げぎんなんを添える。
かつおだしを火にかけ、うすくち醤油、みりんで味をととのえる。椀に注ぎ、三つ葉の軸のみじん切りとぶぶあられを散らす。

一九ページ
本ししゃものフライ

本ししゃもを塩水にくぐらせ、小麦粉をまぶして揚げる。その際、箸でししゃもをつかんだまま腹下のヒレを油に浸け、揚げ固まってから、放つ。

二一ページ
花びら酢がき

まがきの殻を開け、身をはずす。
身を殻にのせ、スプーンでくずした土佐酢ゼリー（一一四ページ「トマトのところてん」参照）をかける。食用花（ベゴニアの改良種）をたっぷりとのせる。

二二ページ
えびいもの熟成焼き

えびいも（2〜3か月熟成させたもの）を皮付きのまま半分に切り、大きさをみて縦に3〜4等分する。蒸し器で蒸して、芯まで火を通す。
鍋に並べ、すっかりかぶるまでかつおだしを加える。弱火でことこと炊いて、だしを煮含める。こいくち醤油、砂糖、みりんで濃い目に味をつけ、火を止め、追いがつおをしてそのまま冷ます。冷蔵庫に移し、1週間ねかせる。
提供時に取り出して水気をぬぐい、薄力粉をうすく、しっかりつけて揚げる。
揚げたいもの油をきり、串打ちする。直火であぶり、表面を乾いた感じに仕上げる。ほうじ茶の茶葉をたっぷりと敷いた大鉢に盛る。

二四ページ
かぶの風呂炊き
ゆず味噌餡

[かぶの風呂炊き]
かぶの皮をむき、六方にむく。鍋に入れ、かぶだしを加えて火にかける。やわらかくなるまで煮て、味を含ませる。

[ゆず味噌餡]
　小麦粉　100g
　バター　65g
　豆乳　1L
　玉味噌（一一三ページ）　500g
　ゆずの搾り汁　2個分
小麦粉をバターで炒めて粉気をぬき、豆乳を（何度かに分けて）加え、かき混ぜながら煮てベシャメルをつくる。

すり鉢に玉味噌を入れ、ベシャメルを1/3量ずつ加えながらすり混ぜる。ゆずの搾り汁を加える。

[仕上げ]
炊いたかぶ1個を器に盛り、適量のゆず味噌餡を鞍がけする。味噌の表面をバーナーであぶる。ゆず皮のすりおろしをふりかける。

二五ページ
香箱がにの薬膳飯蒸し

[香箱がに]
香箱がにを蒸す。甲羅をはずし、身、外子、内子を取り出す。身をほぐし、それぞれに少量のこいくち醤油をふってなじませる。

[薬膳飯蒸し　約25人分]
　もち米　1合
　黒米　1合
　酒　120ml
　塩　少量
　炒った松の実　適量
　しょうがの搾り汁　適量
黒米ともち米を合わせてひと晩浸水する。
水をきり、蒸す。15分間蒸したら酒と塩をふりかけ、さらに15分間蒸す。仕上がりに炒った松の実としょうがの搾り汁を混ぜる。

[仕上げ]
器に飯蒸しを盛り、かにの身、内子、外子の順に重ねる。バーナーで軽くあぶって香りを出した甲羅をかぶせる。

二八ページ
ぶり大根

ぶりを三枚におろし、皮を引く（血合いは残したまま）。さらしで包み、4〜5日間ねかせる。
血合いをはずし、漬け地（こいくち醤油、酒、みりんを同量ずつ合わせて煮切ったもの）に30〜40分間漬ける。刺身に切る。
ビーツの皮をむき、極薄にスライスする。甘酢（一一三ページ）に漬ける。ざくろの実も別に甘酢に漬ける。
ぶりの大きさに合わせて、ビーツをカットする。ぶりとビーツを1枚ずつ交互に並べて器に盛る。ざくろを散らす。

三〇ページ
鰆のたたき
海苔酢

[さわら]
さわらを三枚におろす。さらしで包んで数日間（脂のり具合に合わせて）ねかせる。
串打ちをして、ガス火で皮目をあぶる。冷蔵庫に入れて冷やす。刺身に切る。

[海苔酢　仕上がり約700ml]
　生のり　60g（よく絞ったもの）
　こいくち醤油　180ml
　米酢　180ml
　かつおだし　180ml
　砂糖　120g
　葛　少量
生のりをよく絞る。葛以外の材料を鍋に合わせ、煮る。水溶きした葛を加え、とろみがついたら火を止める。

あえる。脂ののっているものは2～3分間おいてから、器に盛る。

三四ページ
初がつお
わさびの茎の醤油漬け
わさびの花　おろしわさび

1kg大の1本釣りの初夏のかつおを使用。三枚におろして皮を引き、厚めに刺身に切る。
器に重ね盛りにする。わさびの茎の醤油漬け（わさびの茎を洗ってきざみ、こいくち醤油2と米酢1の割合で合わせた地に漬け込んだもの）を散らす。わさびの花を天に盛り、おろしわさびを添える。

三一ページ
さんまの肝あえ
とびこ　青ねぎ　炒りごま

さんまを三枚におろす。肝を取り分ける。
さんまの肝に田舎味噌を合わせ、適量の酒、みりんでのばして加熱しながら練り混ぜ、肝味噌ソースをつくる（一二二ページ「さんまの朴葉焼き」参照）。
さんまの身を約1cm幅に切り、肝味噌ソースで軽くあえて平皿に並べる。とびこ、青ねぎのみじん切り、炒りごまをのせる。

三二ページ
あおりいかインパクト
フルール・ド・セル

6kg大のあおりいかを使用。掃除をした身をさらしに包み、約1週間熟成させる。
深めに蛇腹包丁を入れ、ひとくち大に切り分ける。器に盛り、フルール・ド・セルを添える。

三五ページ
すずきの造り
塩すだち

すずきを三枚におろし、皮を引く。厚さを不揃い気味にして、刺身に切る。
すだちを極薄くスライスし、粗塩をふって軽くもむ。すずきとこの塩すだちを重ね盛りする。食用花（ベコニアの改良種）を散らす。

三三ページ
熟成くろむつの土佐醤油あえ

くろむつを三枚におろし、皮を引く。さらしで包み、（脂ののり具合に合わせて）1週間前後熟成させる。
やや厚めに切り出し、土佐醤油（一一三ページ）で

三六ページ

いさきと鯵の混ぜ造り

みょうが　花穂じそ

脂ののったいさきを三枚におろし、皮を引く。強め
に塩をふり、約20分間おいて身を締める。

あじを三枚におろし、皮を引く。塩をふり、約20分
間おく。

いさき、あじをそれぞれを細造りにして混ぜ、土佐
醤油(一一三ページ)ととびこであえる。

皿に盛り、みょうがのせん切り、花穂じそをたっぷ
りと散らしかける。

四一～四三ページ

フォワグラ最中

[フォワグラの西京漬け]
　フォワグラ
　白こし味噌　2kg
　砂糖　500g
　酒　180ml
　みりん　180ml

フォワグラを注意深く切り開き、内部の血管を掃除
する。元の形に戻す。

白こし味噌に砂糖、酒、みりんをよく混ぜ、味噌床
の地をつくる。約1/3量を容器に敷き詰める。その
上にガーゼを広げてフォワグラを並べ、ガーゼで包
む。上から残りの味噌地を流し入れ、もう1枚のガー
ゼでその表面を覆う。味噌とフォワグラが隙間なく
密着するよう、手でしっかりと押す。

容器に蓋をして冷蔵庫に入れ、1～2週間(季節や
大きさによる)漬け込む。

[フォワグラの火入れ]
フォワグラを味噌床から取り出し、専用フィルムに

入れて真空パックし、湯煎にして(コンベクション
オーブンで47℃設定)40～60分間加熱する。氷水
にあてて冷ます。

棒状に切り分けてオーブンペーパーで包み、断面が
4cm四方のスティック状になるよう、手で押さえて
形を整える。厚さ約5mmに切り分ける。

[具1・白いんげん豆と奈良漬け]
白いんげん豆をひと晩水に浸けてもどし、ゆでる。
湯をきって粗くつぶす。
奈良漬けは5mm角にきざむ。

[具2・栗の渋川煮としば漬け]
栗の渋川煮を粗くつぶす。
しば漬けは5mm角にきざむ。

[具3・干しいもと新しょうが甘酢漬け]
干しいもを刃叩きし、練ってやわらかくする(かた
い場合は、シロップをふりかける)。
新しょうがの甘酢漬けは5mm角にきざむ。

[具4・きざみ干し柿といぶりがっこ]
干し柿の外側のかたいところを細かくきざみ、やわ
らかい果肉に混ぜ込む。
いぶりがっこは5mm角にきざむ。

[仕上げ]
フォワグラのカット、季節のペースト、アクセント
の漬けものを最中の皮2枚で挟む。和紙の専用小袋
に入れてシーリングする。

四五ページ

すっぽんと松茸のスープ

[すっぽんだし]
　すっぽん　2匹
　昆布　15cm
　しょうが　厚めのスライス1枚
　水　4.42L
　酒　1.8L

すっぽんをおろして、薄皮をはぐ。身の周囲にある
脂肪を切り除く。

掃除した身と甲羅を水洗いして、昆布を敷いた鍋に入れる。水を注ぎ、しょうがの薄切り、酒を加えて強火で加熱する。沸騰したら火を弱め、アクを除きながら1時間半〜2時間煮る。
漉して、だしと身に分ける。

[仕上げ]
すっぽんの身を5mm角に切る。人数分のだしと身を鍋にとって温め、夏は塩、冬場は少量の醤油で調味する。しょうがの搾り汁を加える。
松茸の薄切りを軽くあぶる。椀にスープを入れ、松茸を加える。

四六ページ
すっぽん雑炊

すっぽんの身（だしをとるために煮たもの）を、さいの目に切り分ける。
人数分のすっぽんだしと身を鍋にとり、火にかける。白飯を加えて軽く煮る。うすくち醤油と塩少量で味をととのえ、卵でとじて火を止める。
椀に盛り、あさつきの小口切りをたっぷりとのせる。

四七ページ
すっぽんのおこげ

すっぽんの身（火入れしたもの）を5mm角に切る。
野菜（紅芯大根、にんじん、九条ねぎ、なすなど季節の野菜）を掃除して、適宜の大きさ、薄さに切る。
人数分のすっぽんだしと身を鍋にとり、野菜を入れて煮る。野菜に火が通ったらこいくち醤油で味をととのえ、葛引きして、火を止める（野菜餡）。
器におこげ（中国料理用）を盛り、野菜餡をかける。

四八ページ
すっぽんまんじゅう

[生地　16個分]
　小麦粉　300g
　ドライイースト　5g
　ベーキングパウダー　10g
　砂糖　40g
　竹炭パウダー　ごく少量
　熱湯　150ml＋適量
粉類をボウルに合わせ、熱湯を加え混ぜて生地にする（生地がかたければ熱湯を足す）。ラップフィルムをかけ、温かい場所に約1時間おいて発酵させる。

[具　16個分]
　すっぽんの身　1匹分
　下仁田ねぎ　10本
　こいくち醤油　適量
　黒こしょう　適量
　おこわ（蒸したもち米）　適量
火を入れたすっぽんの身を5mm角に切る。
下仁田ねぎを適宜にきざみ、やわらかくなるまで炒めておく。
ボウルにすっぽんとねぎを入れ、こいくち醤油と黒こしょうで調味する。その約半量のおこわを加え混ぜる。

[仕上げ]
発酵させた生地を16個に分割して、小さく丸め、具を包む。蒸し缶に並べて蒸し上げる。

四九ページ
すっぽんラーメン

すっぽんだしを火にかけ、下ゆでしたたけのこ、九条ねぎ、しょうがの薄切りを入れ、数分間煮る。こ

いくち醤油で味をととのえる。

中華めんをゆでて湯をきり、椀に入れる。上記の野菜入りスープを注ぐ。白こしょうをふる。

五〇～五三ページ
デンタッキー

[手羽先ぎょうざ]

朝挽きの鶏の手羽先を使う。骨を抜き、袋状になったところに具（以下参照）を詰め、口を楊枝で止める。塩をふり、1時間半～2時間おいて、水分をぬく。これに小麦粉をまぶし、180℃で揚げる。油をきり、サラマンダーで表面をあぶって、パリッと仕上げる。

[具1・あかざえびと木の芽　餃子1個分]
　あかざえび　1～1.5尾
　木の芽　2枚
　塩　少量
あかざえびの殻をむき、身を包丁で刃叩きする。木の芽、塩を加えてあえる。

[具2・黒米の薬膳蒸し　餃子 約35個分]
　黒米　1合
　もち米　1合
　高麗人参　50g
　酒　120ml
　塩　少量
　松の実（炒る）50g
　くこ　70g
　しょうがの搾り汁　適量
黒米ともち米を合わせ、ひと晩水に浸けて、ザルにあげる。高麗人参を細かくきざんで酒に混ぜる。
もち米をさらしで包んで、蒸し缶で蒸す。15分間たったら、高麗人参入りの酒と塩をふりかけ、さらに15分間蒸す。
蒸し上がりに、松の実、くこ（酒で洗う）、しょうがの搾り汁を加え混ぜる。

[具3・スパイシー飯蒸し　約18個分]
　もち米　1合
　アーモンド（炒ってくだく）　50g
　クミンとガラムマサラ　合わせて3g

　レーズン　50g
蒸したもち米と、その他の材料を混ぜる。

[具4・インカポテトとトリュフ　すべて適量]
　インカのめざめ
　黒トリュフ
　塩
インカのめざめをゆで、皮をむいて、粗くつぶす。きざんだトリュフ、塩を混ぜる。

五四ページ
季節のサラダ

[準備]

にんじん、トマト：甘酢（一一三ページ）に漬ける。
ビーツ：薄切りにして番茶でゆでたのち、甘酢に漬ける。
ごぼう：下ゆでしてから、かつおだし（こいくち醤油、乾燥とうがらしを加える）で煮る。
からすえんどう：かつおだしでゆでる。
きくいも：薄切りして素揚げする。
茎ブロッコリ、野蒜、芽きゃべつ：それぞれ素揚げする。
インカのめざめ：蒸したのち、揚げる。さらにサラマンダーで表面をパリッとさせる。
ルーコラの花芽：サラマンダーで焼く。
サラダ菜（マスタードグリーン、マスタードパープル、わさび菜、ロメインレタス、みず菜など）：掃除して水に浸けてしゃきっとさせ、ペーパーなどで水気をとる。
食用花：色合いをみて、取り合わせる。

[仕上げ]

すべての野菜を器に取り合わせる。食用花も盛る。こまかくきざんだ塩昆布を散らし、少量の太白ごま油であえる。

六〇ページ
時鮭
万願寺とうがらし　赤葉玉ねぎ

時鮭を三枚におろす。身側に軽く塩をふり、1〜2日間ねかせる（塩漬けではないので、塩分はごく軽めに。軽く水分を抜いて旨みを凝縮させるととともに、臭みを抜く）。
身を切り分け、串打ちして皮目から焼く。皮をパリッと、身をふっくらと焼き上げる。
万願寺とうがらし、赤葉玉ねぎ（青い部分、根の部分）をそれぞれ素揚げにして塩をふる。鮭と盛り合わせる。

六一ページ
干し鮎焼き
うるかのパテ　たで蒸しパン

[干し鮎]
鮎を開きにして、塩をふり、風干しする。

[うるかのパテ]
　うるか（鮎の肝を1週間以上塩漬けしたもの）　200g
　卵黄　15個
　酒　360ml
材料を鍋に合わせ、加熱しながら練り合わせる。ミキサーにかけてなめらかにしたのち、容器に流して冷蔵庫に入れる。

[たで蒸しパン]
　米粉　240g
　小麦粉　240g
　ベーキングパウダー　10g
　水　480ml
　きび糖　120g

　たで　16g
粉類を合わせてふるい、ボウルに入れる。
たでの葉を配合の水の半量とともにミキサーにかける。残り半量の水できび糖を溶かしてミキサーに加え、さらに混ぜる。
このたでシロップを粉のボウルに加え混ぜる。大きなダマはつぶしておく。ラップフィルムをかけて温かい場所に約30分間置く（ぷつぷつと泡が出てくるまで）。深めのバットにクッキングシートを敷き、生地を流す。蒸し缶に入れ、約20分間強火で蒸す。

[仕上げ]
干し鮎を焼く。真二つに切る。
蒸しパンを適当な大きさにちぎり、サラマンダーで軽く焼いて、表面をカリッとさせる。鮎を器に盛り、蒸しパンとうるかのパテを添える。

六二ページ
さんまの朴葉焼き
肝味噌ソース
にこにこ銀杏　クスクスと雑穀のトースト
おばけさつまいも

[さんまの下処理]
1尾300g大のさんまを三枚におろして、肝をはずす。
身に塩をして、半日風干しする。

[肝味噌ソース]
　さんまの肝　15尾分
　田舎味噌　30g
　酒　100ml
　みりん　100ml
材料を鍋に合わせ、混ぜながら加熱して、適度な濃度になるまで煮詰める。

[クスクスと雑穀のトースト]
使用するクスクスの1.5倍量のかつおだしを鍋に入れて火にかける。沸騰したら火を止め、クスクスを入れ、蓋をして蒸らす。水分を吸収したら、バターで炒めて、カリカリに仕上げる。
そばの実と麦をそれぞれ炒る。

[仕上げ]
風干ししたさんまの半身を2つに切り分け、串打ちして、皮面のみを熱源にさらして焼く。
朴葉に盛り、肝味噌ソースをたっぷりとぬる。そのままサラマンダーに入れて軽くあぶる。クスクス、そばの実、麦、あさつきの小口切りをたっぷりとのせる。さつまいものチップス（薄切りして素揚げし、軽く塩をふる）と炒りぎんなんを添える。

六四ページ
鱚の一夜干し
海苔酢　松茸のあぶり　すだち

[鱚の一夜干し]
鱚を三枚におろす。身に軽く塩をふり、さらしで包んで約4日間熟成させる。
使う当日、塩をふって半日置く。

[仕上げ]
鱚の身を切り分け、串打ちして焼く。器に盛り、皮に海苔酢（三〇ページ「鱚のたたき」参照）をぬる。薄切りした松茸を片面だけさっとあぶって、海苔酢の上に並べる。すだちを添える。

六五ページ
ブイヤベース
はも　あかざ海老　冬瓜

[ベースのスープ　約30人分]
　かつおだし　5.4L
　玉ねぎ　4個
　トマト　大5個
野菜を適宜な大きさに切る。かつおだしと野菜を鍋

に合わせ、玉ねぎの甘みが出るまで軽く煮る。漉す。

[ブイヤベース　2人分]
　はも　2カット
　あかざえび　1尾
　ほたて貝　2個
　冬瓜　2カット
　赤パプリカ　1/4個
　ベースのスープ　300ml
はもをおろして骨切りし、5～6cm幅に切り分ける。
あかざえびを掃除して、殻ごと縦半分に切る。
ほたて貝を蒸し、貝柱を殻からはずす。貝の汁は集めておく。
冬瓜を切り整え、だし（かつおだしと鶏のだしを合わせる）で煮る。
赤パプリカを直火で焼いて皮を焦がし、むく。ミキサーにかけてピュレ状にして、裏ごしする。
人数分のベースのスープを沸かし、赤パプリカのピュレを加える。ほたて貝柱とその汁、煮た冬瓜を入れて約10分間煮る。はもとあかざえびを加え、さっと煮る。塩で味をととのえ火を止める。
椀に盛り、しょうがの搾り汁、ゆず皮のすりおろしを加える。

六六ページ
甘鯛の揚げ焼き
焼き黒きゃべつ

甘鯛を、うろこをつけたまま二枚におろし、塩をふる。さらしに包み、5日間熟成させる。
適宜の大きさに切る。皮をはずし、身は串打ちをして、ふっくらと焼き上げる。皮は小麦粉をふって約250℃の油で揚げてうろこを立てる。軽く塩をふる。
皿に焼いた甘鯛を盛り、黒きゃべつ（サラマンダーに入れて、パリパリに乾かしたもの）をのせる。うろこを立てた皮を重ねる。

六七ページ

えぼだいの一夜干し

根セロリのピュレ　まぐろ酒盗ソース
赤かぶチップ

［えぼだいの一夜干し］
えぼだいを三枚におろし、塩をふって、一夜干しにする。

［根セロリのピュレ］
　根セロリ　1個
　バター　100g
　水　少量
　塩　少量
根セロリの皮をむいて適宜に切り分ける。水、塩、バターとともに鍋に入れ、落とし蓋をしてやわらかくなるまで煮る。これをフードプロセッサーにかけ、裏ごしする。

［まぐろの酒盗ソース］
　まぐろの酒盗　500g
　酒　360ml
　卵黄　15個
　かつおだし　適量
まぐろの酒盗、酒、卵黄を合わせ、中火にかけて練りあげる。生地がかたくなるので、適宜かつおだしを加えて濃度を調整する。

［仕上げ］
えぼだいの一夜干しを焼く。アルミ皿にとり、根セロリのピュレをたっぷりとのせる。まぐろ酒盗ソースを少量かけ、サラマンダーで焼き色をつける。皿に盛り、赤かぶの薄切りの素揚げを添える。

六八ページ

金華豚の煮焼き

水なすの素揚げ

［金華豚の煮豚］
金華豚の肩ロースを鍋に入れ、かつおだしとこいくち醤油を6対1の割合で加える（肉がすっかり浸かるように）。適量のねぎ、しょうがを加え、やわらかくなるまで弱火（75℃）で、約3時間煮る。
引き上げて、網にあげる。
提供時に大きめのブロックに切り分け、サラマンダーに入れて表面を香ばしく仕上げる。

［揚げなす］
水なすを切り分け、素揚げする。塩をふる。

［仕上げ］
器にとうもろこしの皮（ゆでたのち、オーブンで乾かしたもの）をのせ、金華豚と揚げなすを盛り合わせる。タイム、ローズマリー、セージを添える。肉にフルール・ド・セルをふりかける。

六九ページ

サーロイン牛の焼きしゃぶ

なすの焼き浸し　辛味大根おろし

なすを網焼きし、皮をむいて冷ます。かつおだしを沸かしてうすくち醤油、みりんで味をととのえる。だし地が冷めたらなすを浸し、追いがつおをして1日おく。
なすを取り出し、縦半分に切ってサラマンダーで温める。断面に縦に切り込みを入れ、辛味大根おろし（醤油で味をつけたもの）をたっぷりと盛る。
牛サーロインの薄切りになすをかぶせ、表面をバーナーであぶる。仕上げに土佐醤油（一一三ページ）

を刷毛でぬり、ゆず皮のすりおろしをふる。

七一ページ
いのしし肩肉のロースト
血入り味噌ソース　根菜のチップス

[いのしし肩肉のロースト]
いのしし肩肉の塊に塩をふり、状態をみて数日〜1週間ねかせる（入荷時は肉がかたいので）。
肉の表面は切りはずし、中心部を使う。粒塩をふりかけ、約1時間ねかせる。
油を引いたフライパンで表面を焼き、きれいに色づける。サラマンダーに入れ（中程度の温度帯）、ときどき肉の向きを変えながら、約1時間かけてローストする。

[ソース]
　田楽味噌（一一三ページ）　適量
　かつおだし　適量
　いのししの血と焼き汁　各適量
田楽味噌を鍋にとり、いのしし肉の切り口から出た血、ローストしている間に出た焼き汁を加え、適量のかつおだしを加えて溶きのばしながら弱火で加熱する。塩で味をととのえてソースとする。

[仕上げ]
肉を皿に盛り、ソースをかける。ごぼうときくいものチップス（極薄にスライスして低温から素揚げしたもの）を添える。

七四ページ
鴨葱のブイヨン仕立て
かぶだし

鴨ロースを厚めに切り分け、葛粉をまぶす。
鍋にかぶだし（七二ページ）を張り、鴨肉、ねぎを入れて火にかける。鴨に火が通ったら、うすくち醤油、塩で味をととのえ、火を止める。器に盛り、ゆず皮のすりおろしを加える。

七六ページ
かぶと香箱がに

[かぶの煮物]
かぶを六方にむく。
むいたかぶと皮を鍋に入れ、かつおだしを張る。うすくち醤油、みりん、塩で吸い地加減に味をととのえ、落とし蓋をしてかぶの味が出るまで約20分間、弱火でことことと煮る。だしを漉す。

[かぶだしの餡]
かぶを煮ただしを鍋にとり、火にかける。塩で味をととのえ、水溶きの葛粉を加えてとろみをつける。

[仕上げ]
椀にかぶを盛り、蒸した香箱がに（身、外子、内子）をのせ、ぶだしの餡をかける。

七七ページ
根菜のくず餡

7〜8種類の根菜（紫にんじん、パースニップ、大根4種、金時にんじん）をそれぞれ掃除して、切り整える。鍋に入れ、かつおだしを張る。しょうがの薄切りを加えて根菜がやわらかくなるまで煮る。
提供時に人数分の根菜と煮汁を鍋に取り分け、火にかける。うすくち醤油で味をととのえ、水溶きの葛粉を加えてとろみをつける。

七八ページ
牛ほほ肉の薬膳うしお仕立て

[牛ほほ肉]
牛ほほ肉を鍋に入れ、水をかぶるまで加える。適量のにんにく、ねぎ、しょうがを加えて火にかける。沸騰したら弱火にして、約24時間かけてやわらかくなるまで煮る。引き上げる。
肉を鍋に入れ、かつおだしをかぶるまで加える。うすくち醤油と塩で味をつけ弱火で3〜4時間煮る。火から下ろし、だしに浸けたまま最低一日ねかせ、よく味を含ませる。

[仕上げ]
牛ほほ肉を浸けただしを、ペーパーで漉す。
肉を、大きめに切り分ける。人数分の肉とだしを鍋に入れて火にかけ、沸騰したら適量のくこの実、ローストした松の実、たっぷりの新玉ねぎの薄切り（水にさらしたもの）を加えてさっと火を通す。塩で味をととのえる。
仕上げにねぎのせん切りを盛る。

七九ページ
豚肩ロースとすぐきの椀

[豚肩ロースの煮込み]
豚の肩ロースの塊に塩をふり、すりこむ。鍋に入れる。かつおだしをかぶるまで加え、適量のうすくち醤油、塩、しょうが、ねぎを入れ、3〜4時間かけて弱火で（75℃）煮る。火からおろし、そのままだし地に浸けて味を含ませる。

[仕上げ]
肉を大きめに切り分ける。人数分の肉と煮汁を鍋にとり、火にかける。沸騰したらすぐき菜を加え、軽く煮る。塩で味をととのえる。

椀に肉を盛り、炒りごま、あさつきの小口切りをたっぷりとのせる。だしを注ぎ、黒七味をふる。

八五ページ
みすじごはん

[みすじ肉のお浸し]
　牛みすじ肉（肩内側のやわらかい部位）1本（約4kg）
　かつおだし　2.16L
　みりん　360ml
　こいくち醤油　360ml
　香味野菜（長ねぎの青い部分などのくず野菜、しょうが）　適量
　かつお削り節（追いがつお用）　2〜3つかみ
牛みすじ肉を1個300〜400g大のブロックに切り分ける。油を引いたフライパンで表面を軽く焼き固めておく。
肉以外の材料を鍋に合わせて火にかけ、沸騰したら火を止め、70℃ほどまで冷ます。肉を入れ、55℃を保って約5時間煮る。火からおろしたら、煮汁に浸けたまま冷ます。容器に移し、追いがつおをして冷蔵庫で1週間ねかせる。

[だしごはんの配合　2人分]
　米　1合
　かつおだし　180ml
　うすくち醤油　20ml

[仕上げ　2〜3人分]
　みすじ肉のお浸し　1個
　おろしわさび　適量
土鍋でだしごはんを炊く。火を止めて約10分蒸らす。その間に肉のお浸しを温める。
ごはんが炊き上がったら肉をのせ、蓋をかぶせて蒸らす。客前でプレゼンテーションしてから肉を取り出して切り分ける。だしごはんを茶碗によそって肉を並べ、おろしわさびを添える。

八六ページ

富士山麓きのこごはん

[きのこのコンフィの仕込み]
天然きのこ（今回はヤマドリダケモドキ、アカヤマ
ドリ、コガネヤマドリタケ、オオモミタケ、イロガ
ワリを使用）を掃除する。
たっぷりの白絞油を火にかけ、きのこを入れて、約
60℃を保って30分間加熱する。火からおろし、油に
浸けたまま冷ます。油ごと容器に移して保管する。

[仕上げ]
土鍋でだしごはんを炊く（一三六ページ「みすじご
はん」参照）。
きのこのコンフィをソテーする。ごはんの炊き上が
りにのせて、蒸らす。

八七ページ

いくらごはん

[いくらのお浸し]
海水濃度の塩水を50℃に温め、すじこを浸す。薄皮
がむけてくるので、水洗いする。何度か繰り返し、
完全に薄皮を除く。
ばらばらになったいくらを、かつおだしの地（うす
くち醤油で濃い目に味をつける）に浸す。追いがつ
おをして1日置く。

[仕上げ]
土鍋でだしごはんを炊く（「みすじごはん」参照）。
蓋を開けていくらのお浸しをたっぷりとのせる。

八八ページ

サーロインごはん

土鍋でだしごはんを炊く（「みすじごはん」参照）。
おこげができるよう、最後の1分間は強火にする。
火を止めて、5〜6分間蒸らしてから蓋を開け、牛
サーロインのスライスを生のままのせる。客前で一
度プレゼンテーションする。
蓋をはずして土鍋ごとサラマンダーに入れ、約1分
間表面を焼く。杓文字で肉をちぎりながらごはんと
よく混ぜ、牛の脂をごはんによくなじませる。茶碗
に盛る。

九〇ページ

かきごはん

かきをバターでソテーする。途中、こいくち醤油を
加えて香りよく仕上げる。
土鍋でだしごはんを炊く（一三六ページ「みすじご
はん」参照）。火を止めて約10分間蒸らしたら、蓋
を開けてソテーしたかきを並べ、焼き汁をかけてす
ぐに蓋をかぶせ、しばらく蒸らす。
かきを杓文字でつぶしながら、身とそのジュースを
ごはんによく混ぜこみ、茶碗に盛る。

九二ページ
ポルチーニごはん

[ポルチーニのもどし]
乾燥ポルチーニを洗い、適量の水とともに火にかける。沸いたらアクを除き、火を止めてそのまま冷ます。冷めたらザルに上げ、もどし汁は取り置く。

[ごはんの配合　2人分]
　米　1合
　ポルチーニのもどし汁　90ml
　かつおだし　90ml
　うすくち醤油　20ml＋適量
　塩　適量
もどし汁とかつおだしを半々にしてごはんを炊く。その際、うすくち醤油でやや濃いめに味つけする。火を止めて約10分間蒸らしてから、もどしたポルチーニをのせる。蓋をかぶせてさらに蒸らす。茶碗に盛り、少量の塩をふる。

九四ページ
ほほ肉ごはん

[牛ほほ肉の煮込み]
　牛ほほ肉　3kg
　（水、ねぎの青い部分、しょうがの薄切り　適量）
　かつおだし　3.6L
　こいくち醤油　600ml
　みりん　600ml
牛ほほ肉をたっぷりの水（ねぎ、しょうがも加える）とともに鍋に入れ、火にかける。弱火で1日煮込んでやわらかくする。取り出す。
鍋にほほ肉、かつおだし、こいくち醤油、みりんを入れ、弱火で約3時間煮る。火からおろし、肉はそのまま煮汁に浸けおく。

[仕上げ]
肉を煮汁から取り出し、細かく裂く。だしごはんを茶碗によそい、ほぐしたほほ肉をのせる。きざんだあさつきと炒りごまをのせる。

九三ページ
白子の雑炊

[白子雑炊　1人分]
　炊いた白飯　100g
　白子（裏ごししたもの）　約20g
　かつおだし　180ml
　塩　少量
　黒こしょう　少量
白飯をかつおだしで煮る（雑炊のやわらかさになるまで）。塩で味をつけ、火を止めて白子を加え、混ぜる（余熱で火を入れる）。器に盛り、黒挽きこしょうをふる。

九五ページ
からすみ雑炊

[からすみ雑炊　1人分]
　炊いた白飯　100g
　かつおだし　180ml
　うすくち醤油　少量
　塩　少量
　卵黄　1個
　からすみの薄切り　好みの量
白飯をかつおだしで煮て、うすくち醤油と塩で味をつける。茶碗によそい、中央をくぼませて卵黄を盛り、周囲にからすみ（表面を軽くあぶって薄く切ったもの）をたっぷりとのせる。

九六ページ
宝石ごはん

[宝石ごはん　2人分]
　好みの根菜のさいの目切り　約カップ1
　米　1合
　かつおだし　180㎜
　塩　少量
　バター　10g

根菜（ここではにんじん、京にんじん、黄にんじん、かぼちゃ、ズッキーニ、ラディッシュを使用）をそれぞれ掃除してさいの目に切る。
上記の材料と合わせてごはんを炊く。

一〇〇ページ
梨のワンショット
カモミールティー

梨を丸ごとアルミ箔で包み、200℃のオーブンで約1時間焼く。皮をむき、ミキサーにかけてピュレにする。少量の日本酒、塩、砂糖を加えて味をととのえ、梨のスープとする。冷やしておく。
カモミールティーを淹れ、ヴァニラビーンズを加える。冷やしておく。
スープをガラスの器に注ぎ、梨の果肉の極小角切りとアリッサムの花を浮かべて提供する。客前で、カモミールティーをスープに注ぎ入れる。

一〇一ページ
ハイビスカスのグラニテ
カシスと紫芽のムース

[グラニテ]
ハイビスカスティーを淹れ、シロップで甘みをつける。ほぼ同量のスパークリングワインを加え、冷凍する。提供時にスプーンでかき取る。

[ムース]
カシスのピュレに紫芽を加えてミキサーで混ぜる。鍋にとり、水でふやかしたゼラチンを加えて溶かす。この生地に卵白、適量の砂糖を加え、ハンドミキサーで泡立てる。

[仕上げ]
グラニテをグラスに半分まで入れ、ムースをかさねる。紫芽を飾る。

一〇一ページ
梨のピンチョス

梨の果肉を小さな円筒形に抜く。甘口の日本酒でマリネする。
串に刺し、梨の皮の小片で飾る。しょうがのコンフィ（しょうがのせん切りをシロップで煮たもの）、フレッシュのタイムをのせ、極小丸に抜いたへべす（柑橘）の皮を添える。

一〇二ページ

夏の白雪

白桃
ココナッツのブランマンジェ
ヨーグルトかき氷
クリームチーズのムース

[ココナッツのブランマンジェ　8〜10人分]
　牛乳　180ml
　砂糖　50g
　板ゼラチン（水でふやかす）　8g
　ココナッツミルク　200g
　生クリーム　100ml
牛乳と砂糖とゼラチンを合わせて火にかけ、温めて
砂糖とゼラチンを溶かす。温かいうちに、ボウルに
入れたココナッツミルクに加え合わせ、氷水をあて
て冷やす。ゆるく固まったら、泡立てた生クリーム
を加え混ぜる。容器に流して冷蔵庫に入れる。

[ヨーグルトのかき氷　8〜10人分]
　プレーンヨーグルト　200g
　牛乳　40ml
　砂糖　50ml
材料を混ぜ合わせて容器に流し、冷凍する。提供時
にスプーンでかいてグラニテ状にする。

[チーズのソース　8〜10人分]
　クリームチーズ　80g
　砂糖　20g
　牛乳　120ml
　生クリーム　80ml
クリームチーズに砂糖を練り混ぜ、なめらかにする。
牛乳を少しずつ加え混ぜ、ゆるめる。最後に生クリー
ムを加え混ぜる。

[仕上げ　8〜10人分]
　白桃（皮をむいてカットする）　3〜4個
器に白桃を盛る。ココナッツのブランマンジェをス
プーンですくってのせ、チーズのソースをかける。
ヨーグルトのかき氷をこんもりと盛る。

一〇三ページ

はっか風味の水羊羹

スパイスシロップ

[はっか風味の水羊羹　約20人分]
　こし餡　1kg
　日本はっかとミネラルウオーターで淹れたハーブ
　ティー　1440ml
　板ゼラチン（水でふやかす）30g
ハーブティーにゼラチンを合わせて火にかけ、ゼラ
チンを溶かす。ボウルに入れたこし餡にこのハーブ
ティーを少しずつ加えて混ぜ合わせる。容器に流し
て、冷やし固める。

[スパイスシロップ]
　ミネラルウォーター　200ml
　きび砂糖　100g
　シナモンスティック　5cm
　ナッツメッグ　適量
　しょうが（薄切り）　20g
　塩　少量
全材料を合わせて火にかけ、砂糖を溶かす。沸騰し
たら火を止め、そのまま冷ます。

[仕上げ]
水羊羹を器に盛り、シロップをかける。フルール・
ド・セルを少量ふりかける。

一〇四ページ

黒いちじくとフォワグラクリーム

[黒いちじくのコンポート]
黒いちじくを赤ワインと砂糖で煮てコンポートにす
る。

［フォワグラクリーム］
火入れしたフォワグラの西京漬け（一一六ページ「フォワグラ最中」参照）にマスカルポーネを混ぜ合わせ、適量の牛乳でのばしてなめらかにする。砂糖で甘みをつける。

［仕上げ］
皿にフォワグラクリームを少量ずつ、何カ所かに盛る。それぞれに少量の黒いちじくのコンポート、生のいちじく果肉を重ねる。煮つめたコンポートの汁を添える。

一〇五ページ
ルバーブのコンポート
すいか　ラムゼリーとアマレットゼリー
花穂じそ　紫芽

［ルバーブのコンポート］
ルバーブを掃除して、適宜の大きさに切る。熱湯でさっとゆでて引き上げ、余熱で火を入れる。甘酢（一一三ページ）に漬ける。

［ラムのゼリー］
　ラム酒　180ml
　砂糖　200g
　水　720ml
　板ゼラチン（水でふやかす）　16g
材料を合わせて火にかけ、温まって砂糖とゼラチンが溶けたら火からおろす。氷水にあてて冷やし固める。

［アマレットのゼリー］
　アマレットリキュール　160ml
　砂糖　160g
　水　720ml
　板ゼラチン（水でふやかす）　16g
材料を合わせて火にかけ、温まって砂糖とゼラチンが溶けたら火からおろす。氷水にあてて冷やし固める。

［仕上げ］
　すいか
　紫芽
　花穂じそ
ルバーブのコンポートとすいかを器に盛り、二種のゼリーをくずしてかける。紫芽、花穂じそを散らす。

一〇六ページ
秋のくだもの、
コワントロー風味
ヨーグルトシャーベット

［秋のくだもの］
シャインマスカット、長野パープルぶどう、洋梨、ざくろをそれぞれ掃除する。洋梨はひと口大に切る。

［ヨーグルトのシャーベット］
　プレーンヨーグルト　1kg
　牛乳　200ml
　練乳　250g
材料を混ぜ合わせ、冷凍庫に入れる。1時間ごとにかき混ぜてなめらかに仕上げる。

［コワントロー風味のくず餡］
　コワントロー　90ml
　水　360ml
　砂糖　70g
　葛粉　適量
コワントロー、水、砂糖を合わせて火にかける。砂糖が溶けたら、水どきした葛を加えてひと混ぜし、火を止める。

［仕上げ］
くだものとヨーグルトを器に盛り、ほのかに温かいくず餡をかける。

一〇七ページ

柿のコンポートと
クリームチーズのムース

黒蜜ソース　ラム酒のゼリー

[柿のコンポート]
　柿
　シロップ（水180ml＋砂糖100g）
柿の皮をむき、八等分する。シロップに浸けて1日
おく（柿がよく熟している場合はそのまま使う）。

[クリームチーズのムース　約8人分]
　クリームチーズ　100g
　牛乳　180ml
　砂糖　30g
　板ゼラチン（水でふやかす）　5g
　生クリーム　70ml
牛乳、砂糖、ゼラチンを合わせて火にかけ、砂糖と
ゼラチンを溶かして火を止める。
これを、ボウルに入れたクリームチーズに加え混ぜ
る（多少ダマが残ってもかまわない）。氷水をあてて
冷やし、固まってきたら、泡立てた生クリームを加
える。冷蔵庫に入れる。

[ラム酒のゼリー]
（一三一ページ「ルバーブのコンポート」参照）

[仕上げ]
器に柿のコンポートを盛り、黒蜜（市販）をかける。
クリームチーズのムースをスプーンですくってのせ、
くずしたラム酒のゼリーをのせる。

一〇八ページ

凍りいちじく、
味噌ベシャメルがけ

[凍りいちじく]
いちじくの皮をむき、赤ワインで煮る。冷まして1
個ずつ凍らせる。

[白みそベシャメル]
　白みそ　250g
　ベシャメル（小麦粉30g、バター50g、牛乳500ml）
　かつおだし　適量
白みそとベシャメルを合わせ、適量のかつおだしを
加えてのばす。

[仕上げ]
凍りいちじくを器に盛り、白みそベシャメルをかけ
る。バーナーで表面を軽く焦がして提供する。

一〇九ページ

ビーツと赤ワインの
レデュクション

ミルクアイス
カシス　花穂じそ　紫芽

ビーツの極薄スライスをハイビスカスティーで煮る。
赤ワインにとカシスピュレを合わせ、紫芽も加えて
煮つめる。
器にミルクアイスクリームを盛り、ビーツをのせて、
ソースをかける。花穂じそと紫芽を散らす。

Basic Recipes

[*katsuo-dashi*]

   800 g *katsuo-bushi*

   5 L water

Boil the water in a pot and add the *katsobushi*. Simmer until the katsuobushi has sunk to the bottom of the pot. Turn off the heat and strain with a fine sieve.

[*tosa*-soy-sauce]

   1.8L soy sauce

   360ml *sake*

   20cm *kombu*

   1 handful *katsuobushi*

Put the soy sauce, sake, *kombu* in a saucepan and heat. When it comes to a boil, turn off the heat then add *katsuobushi*. Rest it for a day and strain with a fine sieve.

[*men-tsuyu* sauce]

   720ml *katsuodashi*

   90ml soy sauce

   90ml *mirin*

   1 handful *katsuobushi*

   juice of grated ginger

Put *katuso-dashi*, soy sauce and *mirin* in a saucepan and heat. When it comes to a boil, turn off the heat then add the *katsuobushi* and allow to cool. Strain it with a fine sieve. Add juice of grated ginger, if preferred.

[Sweet vinegar]

   200ml water

   200ml vinegar

   90g sugar

Mix the ingredients.

[*tosa*-vinegar]

   360ml rice vinegar

   180ml *katsuo-dashi*

   60g sugar

   180ml *mirin*

   180ml light soy sauce

   1 handful *katsuobushi*

Put the rice vinegar, *katsuo-dashi*, sugar and *mirin* in a saucepan and heat. When it comes to boil, turn off the heat and add the *katsuobushi*. Rest it for a day and strain with a fine sieve.

[tempura batter]

In a bowl, mix the flour and cornstarch (ratio 2:1), add an adequate amount of beer and stir.

[*tama-miso*]

   2kg strained *shiro-miso*

   1 egg yolk

   360g sugar

   180ml *mirin*, approx.

   180ml *sake*, approx.

Mix all ingredients in a pan, stir and heat on low flame until smooth (adjust the thickness with *sake* and *mirin*).

[*dengaku-miso*]

   2kg strained *aka-miso*

   15 egg yolk

   1kg sugar

   570ml *mirin*, approx.

   570ml *sake*, approx.

Mix all ingredients in a pan, heat and stir until smooth (adjust the thickness with *sake* and *mirin*).

---

glossary

<u>katuobushi</u> : A cured fillet of bonito. There are 2 types, arabushi (a smoke-dried fillet after being simmered) and karebushi (a fillet matured by mold-coating after being somke-dried). We use a mixture of them— with the blend ratio, where the part of the fillet, the thickness of shaving, depends on the season.

<u>kombu</u> : dried and matured kombu kelp

<u>mirin</u> : sweet cooking rice wine

<u>kudzu starch</u> : a flour of the root of kudzu (Japanese arrowroot)

page 一〇

Tomato *tokoroten*

junsai, passionfruit, basil seed,
tosa-vinegar jelly

[tomato *tokoroten*]
  6 large tomatoes
  3L water
  300ml tomato juice
  60g *tengusa* agar (soaked in water overnight)
Squeeze the water out of the *tengusa* agar. In a pan heat the tomatoes, water and *tengusa* agar. When the liquid thickens, add the tomato juice and stir, then filter it through a sieve. Pour in a container and refrigerate until it sets. Cut with a *tokoroten* cutter like noodles.

[*tosa*-vinegar jelly]
  540ml *tosa*-vinegar (see page 一三三)
  10g gelatin (soaked in water)
Add the gelatin to *tosa*-vinegar, heat until the gelatin is dissolved. Pour in a container, refrigerate to set.

[tomato-vinegar marinade]
  tomatoes
  200ml rice vinegar
  200ml water
  90g sugar
Marinate the sliced tomatoes in the mixed seasoning. Then strain (keep the strained tomatoes to use for "Seasonal salad", page 一四二).

[serving]
Place the *tokoroten* in a bowl. Arrange the *junsai*(water shield), passionfruit seed, basil seed and lightly crushed *tosa*-vinegar jelly on top. Place a lotus leaf on top of a bowl. Drop a small amount of tomato-vinegar marinade onto the leaf.

page 一二

Deep-fried conger and beetroot, *shiso* flavor

Fillet the conger eel and cut it into 3 to 4 pieces. Cut a large beetroot into thin round slices.
Sandwich the conger eel with 2 green *shiso* leaves. Cut the sandwich in half. Dredge with flour, dip in a light tempura batter then deep-fry.

---

page 一三

Hamo cutlet

lightly salted *sudachi* citrus salt

Fillet the *hamo* (pike conger) weighing at least 1kg. Apply "*hone-giri* (technique of cutting the small bones)". Cut the fillet into 4 to 5cm pieces. Dredge in flour, dip in egg wash, coat with breadcrumbs, then deep-fry. Garnish with the round sliced salt-massaged *sudachi* citrus. Sprinkle with Guerande flake salt.

---

page 一四

Urchin, small rice bowl

grated *wasabi*, "sea grape" seaweed

Use 2 *murasaki* urchin per person.
Take out the urchin from the shell. Marinate half of the

urchin in a mixture of soy sauce, *sake* and *mirin* for about 10 minutes. Use the other half raw.

Cook the rice "al dente", then mix the rice with *tobiko* (flying fish roe).

Stuff the shell with the rice and top it with the raw urchin, followed by the marinated urchin. Garnish with freshly grated *wasabi* and *umi-budo* "sea grape" seaweed.

---

page 一五

Japanese yam marinated with *kombu*

crushed okra, "*onsen*" poached egg

Peel the skin of the yam and cut it into super-thin strips. Place the "yam noodles" on a cooking tray laid out with the *kombu* sheet. Sandwich the yam with another sheet of *kombu*. Rest it for half a day.

Serve the marinated yam noodles in a bowl with *onsen* poached egg and crushed okra. Pour the *men-tsuyu* sauce (see page 一三三) and garnish with okra blossoms.

---

page 一六

Urchin and fresh *yuba*, "*bekko-an*" sauce

grated wasabi

[*bekko-an* sauce]

360ml *katsuo-dashi*

20ml soy sauce

20ml *mirin*

15g of sugar, approx.

1tsp. *kudzu* starch (dissolved with a small amount of water), approx.

Heat the *katsuo-dashi*, season it with sugar, *mirin* and soy sauce. Add the *kudzu* starch to thicken and turn off the heat.

[serving]

Place the fresh *yuba* in a small bowl, arrange the raw urchin on top. Pour the *bekko-an* sauce and garnish with grated *wasabi*.

---

page 一七

Anago tempura and eggplant "*hitashi*"

okra sauce, small bits of rice cracker

Fillet the *anago* eel. Dredge it in flour, dip in the tempura batter then deep-fry.

Grill the eggplant and remove charred skin. Soak it in the seasoned *dashi* (ratio of *katsuo-dashi* 1, soy sauce 0.5, *mirin* 0.5).

Crush the okra into small pieces.

Prepare the *bekko-an* sauce (see "Urchin and fresh *yuba*, *bekko-an*" sauce), turn off the heat and allow to cool then add the crushed okra.

Arrange the soaked eggplant in a bowl, top it with the *anago* eel and okra. Sprinkle with *bubu-arare* (small bits of rice cracker).

page 一八
Mushroom "tofu"

awa-fu, *konjak*, ginkgo nut, rice cracker

[mushroom *tofu* : serves 36]
    500g wild mushrooms
    about 500ml *katsuo-dashi*
    1280ml Milk
    180g *kudzu* powder

Clean varieties of mushrooms gathered at foot of Mt. Fuji. Quickly boil in the *katuo-dashi* and drain. Puree the mushrooms in a blender. Mix the *kudzu* starch and milk in a bowl until all the lumps are gone. Add the mushroom puree and stir until the batter is evenly mixed. Pour the puree in a saucepan on low heat. Mix slowly with a spatula until the puree thickens. Pour it into a cooling tray and refrigerate until it sets.

[serving]
Cut the mushroom *tofu* into squares. Coat with powdered starch then deep-fry.
Deep-fry the *awa-fu* (wheat gluten cake with millet) and ginkgo nuts. Simmer the *konjak* in the *katsuo-dashi* seasoned with soy sauce and *mirin*.
Place the mushroom *tofu* in a bowl, arrange *awa-fu*, ginkgo nuts and konjak. Heat the *katsuo-dashi* in a pan and season with light-coloured soy sauce and *mirin* then pour into a *wan* bowl. Garnish with a generous amount of finely chopped *mitsuba* (Japanese chervil) stems and sprinkle with *bubu-arare* (small bits of rice cracker).

page 一九
Deep-fried *hon-shishamo* smelt

Rinse *hon-shishamo* fish in a brine. Dredge with flour then deep-fry. When frying, hold the fish with chopsticks (or other kitchen utensils) and dip the belly fin into the heated oil, when the fin is firmly fried, let the fish slip into the oil.

page 二一
Oyster in vineger with flower petals

Open the oyster shell and take out the oyster.
Put the oyster on a half shell and cover it with crushed *tosa-vinegar* jelly (see page 一三三. "Tomato *tokoroten*"). Garnish generously with an edible begonia flower (improved variety of begonia).

page 二二
Roasted, matured *ebiimo* taro

Leave the skin on the taro (matured for 2 to 3 month) and cut it in half. Then cut it lengthwise into 3 to 4 pieces. Steam it thoroughly.
In a pot, pour plenty of *katsuo-dashi* over the taro and season with soy sauce, *sake*, *mirin*. Simmer on a law heat and let it absorb *dashi*. Turn off the heat, add extra *katsuobushi* and allow to cool. Transfer the taro and dashi into a container and let it rest for one week in refrigerator.
When ready to serve, drain and dry the taro, and coat it lightly but thoroughly with flour, then deep-fry. Drain oil from the taro, put them on skewers, and sear it in a direct flame, until surface is dried. Serve it in a large bowl filled with toasted tea leaves.

page 二四

Turnip *"furotaki"* style

yuzu-miso sauce

[turnip *furotaki*]

Peel the turnips and shape into *"roppo* (hexahedron)". Put the turnips in a pan and pour the turnip-*dashi* (see page 七二) over. Heat until the turnip is tender.

[*yuzu-miso* sauce]
    100g flour
    65g butter
    1L soy milk
    500g *tama-miso* (see page 一三三)
    juice of 2 *yuzu* citrus
In a pan, melt the butter and stir in the flour, add the soy milk a little at a time to make a béchamel sauce.
In a mortar add 1/3 of the béchamel sauce at a time to the *tama-miso*, and mix well. Add the *yuzu* juice and stir until it has completely mixed with the sauce.

[serving]
In a bowl, place one turnip and pour the *yuzu-miso* sauce over it. Sear the *miso* with a kitchen torch. Garnish with *yuzu* zest.

---

page 二五

Kobako crab steamed with black rice

[*kobako* crab]
Steam the *kobako* crab. Take off the shell, then take out the crab meat and both the *sotoko** and the *uchiko**. Flake the crab meat. Season with a small amount of soy sauce.
*sotoko : roe of the crab, carried on the stomach

*uchiko : ovary of the crab, packed inside the shell

[*iimushi* : adequate quantity : serves 25]
    180g sticky rice
    180g black rice
    120ml *sake*
    salt
    roasted pine nuts
    grated ginger juice
Soak the black rice and sticky rice in water overnight. Drain water and steam for 15 minutes. Sprinkle *sake* and salt, steam for another 15 minutes. Mix in roasted pine nuts and ginger juice.

[serving]
On a plate, place the *iimushi* and then top it with the crab meat, the *uchiko* and the *sotoko* in that order. Sear the shell of crab with a kitchen torch to bring out flavor, then lay it on the top like a lid.

---

page 二八

Yellowtail and beetroot

Fillet the yellowtail. Peel off the skin without removing the dark meat. Wrap it in a *sarashi* cotton cloth and rest it for 4 to 5 days.
Remove the dark meat, marinate in the mixture of soy sauce, boiled-down *sake*, *mirin* (1:1:1) for 30 to 40 minutes. Slice it into *sashimi*.
Peel the skin off the beetroot, slice them into ultra-thin slices and soak in the sweet vinegar (see page 一三三) with a pomegranate.
Cut the beets into same size as the yellowtail. Place them alternately on a plate and garnish with the pomegranate.

page 三〇

Seared Spanish mackerel

nori-vinegar sauce

[Spanish mackerel]
Fillet the Spanish mackerel, leaving on the skin. Wrap it in a *sarashi* cotton cloth and let it rest for a few days (depending on the fat of the fish).
Skewer the fish and grill it on a direct flame from the skin side. Cool it in the refrigerator. Slice it into *sashimi*.

[*nori* vinegar]
  20g raw *nori*
  60ml soy sauce
  60ml rice vinegar
  60ml *katsuo-dashi*
  40g sugar
kudzu powder (dissolved with a small amount of water)
Drain liquid from the raw *nori*.
Simmer with soy sauce, rice vinegar, *katuo-dashi* and sugar in a saucepan, add the *kudzu* powder and water mixture to thicken, and turn off the heat.

page 三一

Pacific saury with liver sauce

flying fish roe, chives, toasted sesame

Fillet and gut the *sanma*, pacific saury. Set aside the gut.
To make the "liver sauce" (see page 一四三 "Grilled pacific saury on big leaf").
Slice the fillets into 1cm pieces. Lightly dress it with the liver sauce and place on a flat plate. Garnish with *tobiko* (frying fishe roe), finely chopped chives and roasted sesame.

page 三二

Aori squid impact

fleur de sel

Use a large *aori* squid, about 6kg. Clean it and wrap it in a *sarashi* cotton cloth and mature for one week. Because the *aori* squid has thick flesh, score the surface with a knife before cutting it into bite size pieces. Garnish with fleur de sel (Guerande flake salt) on side of a plate.

page 三三

Japanese bluefish with *tosa*-soy-sauce

Fillet the bluefish. Peel off the skin. Wrap it in a *sarashi* cotton cloth and mature it for about one week (depending on the amount of fat). Cut it into large pieces and dress it with a *tosa-soy*-sauce (see page 一三三). When the fish has a lot of fat, rest it for 2 to 3 minutes before serving.

page 三四

Early summer bonito

wasabi stems marinated in soy sauce
wasabi blossoms, grated *wasabi*

Use an early summer bonito of about 1kg size, caught by pole and line fishing. Fillet the bonito, peel off the skin and cut it into thick slices of *sashimi*. In a dish, pile up the slices. Sprinkle the *wasabi* stems marinated in soy sauce based liquid (washed and minced *wasabi* stems, ratio : soy sauce 2 to rice vinegar 1). Garnish with *wasabi* blossoms on the top and *wasabi* on the side of the dish.

---

page 三五

Sea bass sashimi
lightly salted *sudachi* citrus

Fillet the sea bass and take off the skin. Cut it into uneven sashimi pieces. Slice the *sudachi* citrus as thinly as possible and salt-massage it. In a dish pile the seabass slices with the *sudachi* alternatively. Garnish with an edible begonia flower (improved variety of begonia).

---

page 三六

Grunt and horse mackerel
myoga ginger, *shiso* blossoms

Fillet the grunt and peel off the skin. Sprinkle with plenty of salt and rest it for 20 minutes.
Fillet the horse mackerel and peel off the skin. Sprinkle with salt and rest it for 20 minutes.
Cut the grunt and the mackerel into thin strips and mix with *tosa*-soy-sauce (see page 一三三) and *tobiko* (frying fish roe).
Place it in a bowl. Garnish with *myoga* ginger cut into fine strips and sprinkle a generous amount of *shiso* blossoms.

page 四一—四三

Foie gras *monaka*

[foie gras sweet-*miso* marinate]
  foie gras
  2kg sweet-*miso*
  500g sugar
  180ml *sake*
  180ml *mirin*
  Carefully open the foie gras and de-vein then put it back together.
Mix together sweet-*miso*, *sake*, sugar and *mirin*. Spread 1/3 of this *miso*-mixture in a container. Place a large gauze on the *miso*-mixture. Place the foie gras on the gauze and wrap it completely. Pour the remaining *miso* mixture on the gauce and cover the surface with another gauze. Press down with your hand to make sure the *miso*-mixture covers the foie gras.
Put a lid on the container and marinate in the refrigerator for 1 to 2 weeks (depending on the size and season).

[foie gras]
Take out the foie gras from a container. Place it in a vacuum pack and put into a bain-marie at 47°c for 90 minutes. Cool in an ice water bath.
Cut the foie gras into a few large sticks. Wrap it in parchment paper, and using your hand mold them into sticks of 4cm on all sides. Then cut them into 5mm slices. Sandwich one slice of foie gras and the garnish (paste of the day) between two *monaka*-wafers. Seal in a small *washi* paper bag.

[garnish 1 : white kidney beans & *narazuke* pickle]
white kidney beans : To reconstitute, soak in water overnight. Boil, drain and mash coarsely.
narazuke pickles : cut into 5mm squares.

[garnish 2 : simmered chestnut & *shibazuke* pickle]
simmered chestnut with astringent skin : coarsely mash.
shibazuke pickles : cut into 5mm squares.

[garnish 3 : semi-dried sweet potato & sweet vinegared young ginger]
semi-dried sliced sweet potato : finely chop and mash into

a paste with a knife (if the potato is hard to mash, add syrup).

vinegared young ginger pickles : cut into 5mm squares.

[garnish 4 : chopped dried *kaki* & smoked and dried *daikon* pickle]

dried *kaki* (persimmon) : Finely chop the hard part of the *kaki* and mix with the pulp.

smoked *daikon* radish pickles : cut into 5mm squares.

---

page 四五

Suppon softshell turtle consommé with *matsutake*

[suppon broth]

 2 *suppon*

 15cm *kombu*

 1 thick slice of ginger

 4.42L water

 1.8 L *sake*

Fillet the suppon, take off the skin and remove the fat around the flesh. Rinse the shell with water.

Place *kombu* in a pot, put the *suppon* flesh on top. Add water and thin slices of ginger, then heat it on high temperature. Bring to boil and reduce to low heat and simmer and remove scum for 1.5 to 2 hours. Turn off the heat, filter the broth.

[serving]

Cut *the* flesh of *suppon* into 5mm squares. Put the *suppon* broth and the flesh (adjust the quantity according to the number of guests) into a pan and heat. Season with salt(in summer) or with small amount of soy sauce (in winter) and add the juice of grated ginger.

Lightly grill thin slices of *matsutake*.

Pour the soup into a *wan* bowl and garnish with the *matsutake*.

page 四六

Suppon zosui

Cut precooked *suppon* flesh into cubes.

Put the suppon broth and the flesh (adjust the quantity according to the number of guests) into a pan and heat. Add the cooked white rice and simmer lightly. As the finishing touch, season with light-coloured soy sauce and salt, add beaten egg by pouring it evenly in a circle and turn off the heat. Pour in a *wan* bowl, sprinkle with a generous amount of finely minced Japanese chives.

---

page 四七

Suppon and *okoge*, deep-fried crispy rice

Cut precooked *suppon* flesh into 5mm squares. Clean vegetables (*daikon* radish, carrot, *kujo* scallion, eggplant and other seasonal vegetables) and cut them into same size and same thickness.

Pour the *suppon* broth (adjust the quantity according to the number of guests) into a pan. Add the *suppon* flesh and the vegetables then simmer. When the vegetables are tender, season with soy sauce and add a small portion of *kudzu* starch (dissolved with water). Turn off the heat.

Place deep-fried crispy rice in a bowl, pour on the simmered vegetable sauce.

page 四八

Suppon manju, steamed buns

[dough : serves 16]
   300g flour
   5g dry yeast
   10g baking powder
   40g sugar
small portion of bamboo charcoal
150ml+(as needed) hot water
In a bowl, mix the dry ingredients. Add hot water to make dough (if dough is too hard, add more hot water). Cover with plastic film and leave to prove in a warm place for about one hour.

[filling : serves 16]
   the flesh of 1 *suppon*
   10 *Shimonita* leek
   soy sauce
   black pepper
   steamed sticky rice
Cut the precooked *suppon* flesh into a 5mm squares. Saute the chopped *Shimonita* leek. Mix the *suppon* and *Shimonita* leek in a bowl, season with soy sauce and black pepper. Add about half a portion of sticky rice.

[*manju*]
Divide the dough into 16 pieces. Roll them into small balls. Spread each dough and wrap the *suppon* filling. Just before serving, steam it.

page 四九

Suppon ramen

Heat the *suppon* broth in a pan (adjust the quantity according to the number of guests). Add the boiled sliced bamboo shoots, *Kujo* scallion and thinly sliced ginger. Lightly simmer, season with soy sauce and turn off the heat.

In another pan, boil the Chinese noodles, drain and put into a *wan* bowl. Pour the soup and sprinkle with white pepper.

---

page 五〇 - 五三

Dentucky

[chicken wing dumpling]
Use the wings of freshly slaughtered chicken. Debone the wing, make a pocket and stuff the filling (see below), seal opening with a toothpick. Sprinkle with salt and rest for 1.5 to 2 hours to drain excess moisture from the chicken.
Dredge the chicken dumpling in flour, deep-fry in a 180°C oil. Drain oil and lightly sear in a salamander. Serve crispy.

[filling1 : langoustine with *kinome* (for 1 dumpling)]
   1 to 1.5 langoustine
   2 *kinome* (young bud of Japanese pepper)
   Salt
Take the head off the langoustine and peel. Chop, season with salt and dress with *kinome*.

[filling2 : sticky black rice with *yakuzen* ingredients (for about 35 dumplings)]
   180g black rice
   180g sticky rice
   50g ginseng
   120ml *sake*
   salt
   50g roasted pine nuts
   70g wolfberry
   small amount of juice of grated ginger
Mix the black rice and the sticky rice in a bowl, soak in water overnight. Drain in a strainer.
Chopped the ginseng and soak in *sake*. Wrap the rice in *sarashi* cotton cloth and steam for 15 minutes. Sprinkle the ginseng with *sake* and salt on the rice and steam for another 15 minutes.
Mix the pine nuts, the wolfberry (rinsed in *sake*) and juice

of grated ginger with the steamed rice.

[filling3 : spicy sticky rice with almond (for about 18 dumplings)]

    180g steamed sticky rice

    50g roasted almond

    50g raison

    3g mixture of cumin and garam masala

Add the almond, raison and mixed spices to the steamed sticky rice.

[filling4 : "Inka" potato with black truffle (for 18 dumplings)]

    Inka potato

    black truffle

    salt

Boil the Inka potato then peel off the skin. Smash coarsely in a bowl. Add the chopped truffle and salt.

page 五四

Seasonal salad

[preparation]

carrot, tomato : pickle in sweet vinegar.

beets : slice thinly, boil in *ban-cha* tea, then pickle in sweet vinegar.

burdock : pre boil, simmer in *katsuo-dashi* (seasoned with soy sauce, dry red pepper).

vetch : boil in *katsuo-dashi*.

Jurusalem artichoke : slice thinly and deep-fry.

stick broccoli, wild rocambole, Brussels sprout : deep-fry.

Inka potato : steam and deep-fry, then sear in a salamander.

flower bud of rocket lettuce : sear in a salamander.

variety of green vegetables : (mustard greens, mustard purple, *wasabi* greens, romaine lettuce, potherb mustard etc.) : clean and fully submerge in a bowl of cold water to make vegetables crisp. Dry with paper towel.

[presentation]

Arrange all vegetables in a bowl. Garnish with an edible flower. Sprinkle on chopped salt-*kombu*. Dress vegetables with small amount of non-roasted sesame oil.

page 六〇

Tokisake salmon

manganji pepper, red spring onion

Fillet the *tokisake* salmon. Lightly sprinkle salt on the fillet and let it rest for 1 to 2 days to draw out the water, this increases umami and removes odour.

Cut the fillet and skewer, grill until the skin is crispy and the flesh tender. Deep-fry the *manganji* pepper and red onion. Arrange the vegetables on a plate with the salmon.

page 六一

Grilled lightly-dried *ayu*, sweetfish

uruka pate, *tade* leaf steamed bread

[drying sweetfish]

Butterfly the sweetfish, salt and air dry. Then grill it.

[*uruka* pate]

    200g *uruka* (sweetfish gut salted for more than 1 week.)

    15 egg yolk

    360ml *sake*

Put the *urka*, egg yolk and *sake* in a pan, heat and stir until smooth. Process the paste in a blender until it is completely smooth. Pour into a container and refrigerate.

[steaming *tade* bread]

    240g rice flour

    240g wheat flour

    10g baking powder

    480ml water

    120g cane sugar

    16g *tade* leaf

In a bowl, sift together all the dry ingredients.

Mix the *tade* leaves and 1/2 amount of water in a blender.

Dissolve the cane sugar with the rest of the water then add to the blender, stir.

Add the tade syrup in the bowl, mix and remove any large lumps. Cover with plastic wrap and place it in a warm place for 30 minutes (until it's bubbly on the surface).

In a deep cooking tray lined with parchment paper, pour the batter, and steam on a high heat for about 20 minutes.

[serving]

Cut the steamed bread into pieces. Lightly toast in a salamander to make it crisp on the surface. Cut the grilled fish into half and arrange on a plate with *urka* pate and steamed bread.

---

page 六二

Grilled pacific saury on big leaf

liver *miso* sauce, *roasted* gingko nut, cuscus and grain on toast, sweet potato chip

[*sanma*, pacific saury]

Fillet and gut the saury (size of about 300g). Set aside the gut.

Salt the fillets and air dry for half a day. Skewer and grill from the skin side.

[liver sauce : serves 10]

   saury gut from 10 fish

   10g *inaka miso*

   70ml *sake*

   70ml *mirin*

In a saucepan combine all the ingredients, then stir and heat it until it thickens.

[crispy cuscus and grain]

In a pot, pour the *katsuo-dashi* (1.5 times the amount of cuscus) and heat. Bring to a boil, turn off the heat. Add the cuscus and let it cook covered with a lid. When the cuscus has absorbed the liquid, saute it with butter. Separately toast the buckwheat and barley.

[serving]

Place the grilled saury on a *hoba* leaf, brush on a generous amount of the liver sauce. Lightly warm it up in a salamander. Arrange cuscus, buckwheat, barley and finely chopped Japanese chive on the saury. Garnish with sweet potato chips (sliced, deep-fried and lightly salted) and roasted ginkgo nuts.

---

page 六四

Grilled Spanish mackerel

nori-vinegar sauce, grilled *matsutake*, *sudachi* citrus

Fillet the mackerel. Salt the fillets and wrap in a *sarashi* cotton cloth and mature it for 4 days.

When serving, salt and rest the fish for half a day. Cut the fillets into adequate pieces and grill.

Arrange the fish, skin side up on a plate and brush on the *nori*-vinegar sauce (see page 一三七 "Seared Spanish mackerel") on the skin side.

Lightly grill the sliced *matsutake* on one side and place on the sauce. Garnish with the *sudachi* citrus.

---

page 六五

Bouillabaisse

hamo conger, langoustine, white gourd

[basic soup : serves 30]

   5.4L *katsuo-dashi*

   4 onion

   5 large size tomato

Cut the vegetables to an adequate size. Put them in a pot, add the *katsuo-dashi* and simmer lightly to bring out the sweet flavor of the onion. Run the soup through a strainer.

[ingredients : serves 2]

    2 pieces of *hamo* (pike conger) fillet

    1 langoustine

    2 scallops

    2 pieces of wedges gourd

    1/4 red paprika

    300ml basic soup

hamo : Fillet, apply *hone-giri* (technique of cutting the small bones) then cut into pieces.

langoustine : Clean and cut unpeeled shrimp in half lengthwise.

scallop : Steam and remove from the shell. Set aside the steamed juice.

wedges gourd : Cut into pieces and simmer in the *dashi* (combination of *katsuo-dashi* and chicken broth).

paprika : Char over an open flame, remove charred skin, puree in blender and strain through a fine sieve.

Heat the basic soup (adjust the quantity according to the number of guests). Add the paprika puree, scallops, scallop juice, wedges gourd and simmer for 10 minutes. Add the pike conger, langoustine and after a quick simmer, turn off the heat. Arrange in a bowl. Garnish with the juice of freshly grated ginger and the grated zest of *yuzu* citrus.

---

page 六六

Crispy scale tilefish
roasted black cabbage

Fillet the tilefish without removing the scales and salt it. Wrap in a *sarashi* cotton cloth and mature for 5 days.
Cut the fillets into pieces. Separate the skin and the flesh. Dredge the skin with flour, deep-fry at 250°C to make the scales stand up. Grill the flesh and salt it lightly.
Arrange the flesh on a plate with black cabbage (crisp dried in a salamander), top it with the deep-fried fish skin.

page 六七

Grilled butterfish
celeriac puree, tuna "*shuto*", red turnip chip

[butterfish]
Fillet the butterfish. Salt the fillets and air dry over-night. Then grill it.

[celeriac puree]

    1 celeriac

    100g butter

    water

    salt

Peel the celeriac and cut into pieces. Place in a pot with water, salt and butter. Simmer with *otoshi-buta* (a small lid resting directly on the food). Puree in a blender and strain through a sieve.

[tuna *shuto* sauce]

    500g tuna *shuto* (salted tuna gut)

    360ml *sake*

    15 egg yolk

    katsuo-dashi

In a pan, heat the *shuto*, *sake*, egg yolk and stir constantly until it thickens. Add an adequate amount of *katuso-dashi* to adjust the consistency.

[serving]
Place the grilled butterfish on an aluminnum plate and pour a generous amount of the celeriac puree and a small amount of *shuto* sauce. Sear in a salamander. Arrange the butterfish on a plate. Garnish with deep-fried red turnip chips.

page 六八

Stewed and roasted *Kinka* pork

deep-fried eggplant

[stewing *Kinka* pork]
Place the shoulder roast of *Kinka* pork in a pot. Pour *katsuo-dashi* and soy sauce into a pan in a ratio of 6 to 1 (add enough *dashi* liquid to cover the pork.) Add an adequate amount of scallion and ginger and simmer at low heat (75°C) for 3 hours. Transfer the pork to a wire rack. When serving, cut the pork into large blocks. Sear the surface in a salamander for seared flavor.

[deep-fried eggplant]
Cut *mizu-nasu* (eggplant), then deep-fry. Drain it and season with salt.

[serving]
Place *Kinka* pork and fried eggplant on a skin of a corn (boiled and oven dried). Garnish with thyme, rosemary and sage. Sprinkle with Guerande flake salt.

---

page 六九

Beef sirloin "*yaki-shabu*"

grilled eggplant soaked in *dashi*, grated tangy *daikon*

Grill the eggplant and peel off the skin. Boil the *katuo-dashi*, season with light-coloured soy sauce and *mirin*, turn off the heat and allow to cool. Soak the peeled eggplant in this *dashi*, add the *katuobushi* and let it rest over night.
Take the eggplant out of *dashi* and cut it lengthwise. Heat it in a salamander. Cut a slit lengthwise and top with a generous amount of grated tangy *daikon* radish seasoned with soy sauce. Salt the thinly sliced sirloin beef and arrange on top of the eggplant. Sear the surface with a kitchen torch. Brush on *tosa*-soy-sauce (see page 一三三) and sprinkle the grated *yuzu* zest.

---

page 七一

Roasted wild boar shoulder

miso "salmi" sauce, root vegetable chip

[roasting wild boar shoulder]
Salt-marinate the wild boar shoulder and let it rest for few days to a week (the meat can be tough when purchased).
Cut away the surface and use the meat in the center. Sprinkle with coarse salt and rest it for one hour.
Heat the oil in a frying pan and heat the meat until golden brown on all sides, then place in a salamander and roast for one hour, occasionally turning the meat.

[sauce]
　dengaku-miso (see page 一三三)
　katsuo-dashi
　blood of wild boar, roasting juice
　salt
Put the *dengaku-miso* in a saucepan, add the wild boar blood (taken while cutting the boar), roasting juiceand an adequate amount of *katuo-dashi*, heat and stir on a low flame until smooth. Season with salt.

[serving]
Arrange the meat on a plate and pour the sauce. Garnish with the burdock and Jerusalem artichoke chips (sliced and deep-fried starting from a low temperature).

page 七四

"Duck scallion" bouillon

turnip *dahi*

Cut the duck breast into thick slices. Dredge with *kudzu* starch.

Pour the turnip-*dashi* (see page 七二) into a pot, add the duck meat, scallion and turn on the heat. When the duck is heated, season the *dashi*-bouillon with light-coloured soy sauce and salt and turn off the heat. Serve it in a bowl with zest of *yuzu* citrus.

page 七七

Root vegetable with "*kudzu an*" sauce

Clean 7 to 8 varieties of root vegetables (purple carrot, parsnip, 4 varieties of *daikon* radish, red *kintoki* carrot). Cut them into pieces. Place the vegetables in a pot, covered with *katsuo-dashi*, add slices of ginger. Simmer until tender. When serving, reheat the required amount in a pot. Season with light-coloured soy sauce, add a small portion of *kudzu* starch (dissolved with water) to give thickness.

page 七六

Turnip and *kobako*-crab

[simmering turnip]

Peel the skin off the turnip and cut into it "*roppo* (hexahedron)" pieces. Place the turnip and peeled skin in a pot. Add *katsuo-dashi* and simmer on a low heat for 20 minutes. Season with light-coloured soy sauce, *mirin* and salt. Simmer for another 20 minutes with an *otoshi-buta* (small lid resting directly on food). Stir occasionally, let the turnip absorb *dashi*. Strain the *dashi* through a sieve.

[*an* sauce]

Pour the strained *dashi* in a pan and heat and season with salt. Add a small portion of *kudzu* starch (dissolved with water), stir gently and quickly and turn off the heat.

[serving]

Place the simmered turnip in a bowl and top with the steamed *kobako*-crab (crab meat, *sotoko**, *uchiko**). Pour the *an* sauce.

Sprinkle with *bubu-arare* (small bits of rice cracker).

**sotoko* : roe of the crab, carried on the stomach

**uchiko* : ovary of the crab, packed inside the shell

page 七八

"*Yakuzen ushio*" style beef cheek

[beef cheek]

Place the beef cheek in a pot, then add enough water to cover the meat, add an adequate amount of garlic, leek, and ginger. Bring to boil then reduce to a low heat, boil for 24 hours until the meat is tender. Take it out of the pot.

Place the boiled beef into another pot, add enough *katsuo-dashi* to cover. Season with light-coloured soy sauce and salt, simmer for 3 to 4 hours. Turn off the heat and allow to cool and let it rest for at least one day for the beef to absorb the *dashi*.

[serving]

Strain the beef soaked *dashi* with straining paper. Cut the beef into large pieces.

Put the beef (according to the number of guests) and *dashi* in a pan and bring to a boil. Add wolfberry, roasted pine nuts, generous amount of season fresh onion (pre-rinsed in cold water) and heat quickly. Season with salt. Place the beef on a plate and garnish with thin strips of leek.

page 七九
Pork shoulder loin and *suguki* soup

[simmer pork shoulder]

Rub the block of pork shoulder loin with salt. Put it into a pot and add enough *katsuo-dashi* to cover. Add an adequate amount of light-coloured soy sauce, salt, ginger and scallion. Simmer on a low heat for 3 to 4 hours. Remove from the heat, cool the pork to absorb the *dashi*.

[serving]

Cut the meat into large pieces. Strain the pork soaked *dashi* with straining paper.

Put the pork (depending on the number of guests) and the *dashi* in a pan and bring to boil. Add *sugukina* green, and simmer on low heat. Season with salt.

Place the meat in a *wan* bowl, add a generous amount of roasted sesame and Japanese chives. Pour the strained *dashi* and sprinkle with black *shichimi* (chili spice).

---

page 八五
Beef top-blade rice

[beaf "hitashi" for preparation]

  10 or about 3kg beef *misuji*, top-blade
  3.6L *katsuo-dashi*
  600ml *mirin*
  600ml soy sauce
  aromatic vegetables (green part of leek, ginger, vegetables scraps)
  2-3 handful of grated *katsuobushi*

Add oil to a heated frying pan. Place the beef top-blade in the pan and sear until golden brown on all sides. Set aside the beef.

Put all other ingredients in a pot and bring to boil, turn off the heat and cool to 70°C. Add the beef and simmer at 55°C for 5 hours. Remove from the heat and allow to cool in the broth. Transfer the meat and broth into a container and add the extra *katsuobushi* and refrigerate for one week.

[ingredients for *dashi*-rice : serves 2]

  180g rice
  180ml *katsuo-dashi*
  20ml light-coloured soy sauce

[serving]

  1 beef top-blade "hitashi"
  grated *wasabi*

Cook the rice in a *donabe* earthenware pot. Turn off the heat and let the rice steam for about 10 minutes. Place the marinated meat on the rice, put the lid back on and let it steam for a while. Open the lid at the guest's table, then take back to the kitchen. Take out the meat from the pot and slice it.

Serve the *dashi*-rice in a bowl. Arrange the sliced beef on the rice and garnish with grated *wasabi*.

---

page 八六
Mt.Fuji mushroom rice

[mushroom confit]

Clean the wild mushrooms gathered at foot of Mt. Fuji. In a pot, pour a generous amount of a refined canola oil and heat, add the mushrooms and cook in the oil kept at 60℃ for 30 minutes. Remove from the heat and cool the mushrooms in the oil. To preserve, pour into a container with the oil.

[serving]

Cook the *dashi*-rice in a *donabe* earthenware pot (see "Beef top-blade rice"). Saute the mushroom confit. When the rice is cooked, remove the pot from the heat, place the mushrooms on the rice, then put back the lid and let it steam for a while.

page 八七

Salmon roe rice

[marinating salmon roe]

Put the *sujiko* (salmon roe) in a 50°C brine (seawater concentration) and remove the membranes to make *ikura*, the loosened roe.

Soak the loosened salmon roe in *katsuo-dashi* (strongly seasoned with light-coloured soy sauce), and add an adequate amount of *katsuobushi* (to add extra umami) and let it rest for a while.

[serving]

Cook the *dashi*-rice in a *donabe* earthenware pot (see "Beef top-blade rice"). Open the lid and put a generous amount of marinated salmon roe on the rice.

---

page 八八

Beef sirloin rice

Cook the dashi-rice in a *donabe* earthenware pot (see "Beef top-blade rice"). To make an *okoge* (scorched rice), cook the last one minute on a high heat. Turn off the heat and let it steam for 5 to 6 minutes. Place the raw sirloin slices on top of the rice. Open the lid at the guest's table, back to kitchen, put the pot in a salamander and grill it for about one minute. Mix the rice and beef by tearing up the beef into small pieces with a spatula. Serve it in a bowl.

page 九〇

Oyster rice

Saute the oyster with butter. Add soy sauce to enhance the flavour. Cook the *dashi*-rice in a *donabe* earthenware pot (see page 一四七 "Beef top-blade rice"). Turn off the heat and let it steam for 10 minutes. Open the lid and quickly place the oyster on top with the sautéed juice. Put the lid back on and let it steam for a while. Crush the oyster with a spatula, and thoroughly mix oyster, sautéed juice and rice together. Serve it in a bowl.

---

page 九二

Porcini rice

[rehydrating dried porcini]

Wash the dried porcini, immerse in a pan of water. Heat it and bring to boil, skim off the forms and remove from the heat. Let it cool. Drain and set aside the strained liquid.

[porcini rice : serves 2]
    rehydrated dried porcini
    180g rice
    90ml porcini infused liquid
    90ml *katsuo-dashi*
    20ml＋(as needed) light-coloured soy sauce
    salt

Cook the rice with the porcini infused liquid, *katsuo-dashi* and light soy sauce in a *donabe earthenware* pot. Turn off the heat and steam for 10 minutes. Place the porcini on the rice, put back the lid and let it steam for a while. Serve it in a bowl and sprinkle with salt.

page 九三

Milt of cod *zosui*

black pepper

[milt of cod *zosui* rizotto]
  100g cooked white rice
  20g *shirako*, milt of cod (strained through a fine sieve)
  180ml *katsuo-dashi*
  salt
  black pepper

Simmer the cooked white rice in *katsuo-dashi* until soft. Season with salt, turn off the heat, add a *shirako* and mix (cook on residual heat). Serve it in a bowl and sprinkle with black pepper.

page 九四

Beef cheek rice

[simmering beef cheek]
  3kg beef cheek
  (water, green part of leek, thin slices of ginger)
  3.6L *katsuo-dashi*
  600ml soy sauce
  600ml *mirin*

Simmer the beef cheek with plenty of water (add leek and ginger) for a day on low heat until tender. Take out the meat and put in another pot, add *katsuo-dashi*, soy sauce and *mirin*. Simmer for 3 hours. Turn off the heat and allow to cool in *dashi*.

[serving]

Take the beef out from *dashi* and shred. Serve freshly cooked *dashi*-rice in a bowl. Arrange the shredded beef on the rice and garnish with finely chopped Japanese chives and roasted sesame.

page 九五

Bottarga *zosui*

[bottarga rice : serves 1]
  100g cooked white rice
  180ml *katsuo-dasi*
  salt
  light-coloured soy sauce
  1 egg yolk
  bottarga (prefered amount, thinly sliced)

Simmer the cooked white rice in *katsuo-dashi* until soft. Season with light-coloured soy sauce and salt.

Serve it in a bowl. Make a dimple in the middle and drop the egg yolk. Garnish around the egg with a generous amount of sliced bottarga (seared lightly on the surface).

page 九六

Jewelry rice

[jewelry rice : serves 2]
  1 cup of diced root vegetable of choice
  180g rice
  180ml *katsuo-dashi*
  salt
  10g butter

Use a variety of root vegetables (for this recipe : carrot, red carrot, yellow carrot, pumpkin, zucchini, radish). Clean each vegetable and dice. Cook the rice with all the ingredients.

page 一〇〇

Chamomile flavoured Asian pear soup

Wrap an Asian pear in aluminum foil and roast at a 200°C oven for 1 hour. Peel off the skin and puree in a blender. Add small amount of sake, salt and sugar then refrigerate. Make a chamomile tea and add vanilla seeds, then refrigerate.

Pour the pear soup into a glass bowl and add the Asian pears cut into small cubes. Sprinkle sweet alyssum flowers and serve. Pour the chamomile tea into a bowl at the guest's table.

page 一〇一

Hibiscus granite

Cassis and red *shiso* sprout mousse

[granite]
Make hibiscus tea, sweeten it with syrup. Add the same amount of sparkling wine and freeze it. When serving, scrape it with a spoon.

[mousse]
Combine the red shiso sprouts and the cassis puree in a blender. In a pan, pour the puree mixture and gelatin already softened in water, heat until the gelatin is dissolved. Put this mixture in a bowl in an ice-water bath, add egg white and an adequate amount of sugar, whip it with a hand mixer.

[serving]
Fill half a glass with the granite and the top half with the mousse. Garnish with red *shiso* sprouts.

page 一〇一

Asian pear pincho

ginger confit, *hebesu* citrus zest, fresh thyme

Cut the Asian pear with a cylinder shaped cutter. Marinate it with sweet sake.

Skewer the pear. Garnish with small pieces of pear's skin, ginger confit (thin slices of ginger simmered in syrup), *hebesu* citrus zest (cut into a tiny circle) and some fresh thyme.

page 一〇二

Summer snow

white peach, coconut blanc-manger, yogurt shaved ice, cream cheese mousse

[coconut blanc-manger : serves 8 to 10]
   180ml milk
   50g sugar
   8g gelatin (softened in water)
   200g coconut milk
   100ml fresh cream

In a pan, put the milk, sugar and gelatin and heat. When the sugar and gelatin are dissolved, turn off the heat. Combine this warm mixture with coconut milk in a bowl then cool it in an ice-water bath. When cooled and slightly hardened, add whipped cream. Pour into a container and refrigerate.

[yogurt shaved ice : serves 8 to 10]
   200g plain yogurt
   40ml milk
   50g sugar

Mix the ingredients and pour into a container and freeze until set.

When serving, scrape it with a spoon to make a granite.

[cheese sauce : serves 8 to 10]
   80g cream cheese
   20g sugar
   120ml milk
   80ml fresh cream

Mix the sugar into the cream cheese until it's smooth. Add the milk, a small portion at a time then add fresh cream and mix.

[serving]
   white peach (peeled and sliced)

Place the sliced peaches in a bowl. Scoop on the coconut blanc-manger with a spoon. Pour the cheese sauce, and top it with shaved ice.

---

page 一〇三
Japanese mint flavoured red bean jelly
spicy syrup

[mint flavoured *mizu-yokan*]
   1kg strained bean paste
   1450ml herb tea brewed with Japanese mint in mineral water
   30g gelatin (softened in water)

Pour herb tea and gelatin in a pot and heat until gelatin is dissolved. Put the bean paste in a bowl, add the tea, a small portion at a time. Pour into a container and refrigerate.

[spicy syrup]
   200ml mineral water
   100g cane sugar
   5cm cinnamon stick
   20g ginger (thinly sliced)
   nutmeg
   salt

Put all the ingredients in a pan, heat until the sugar is dissolved. Then cool it.

[serving]
Arrange the jelly on a plate and pour the syrup over it. Sprinkle on a small amount of Guerande flake salt.

---

page 一〇四
Black fig and foie gras cream

[black fig puree]
Make a black fig compote with red wine and sugar.

[foie gras cream]
Add mascarpone to the *miso* flavoured foie gras (see page 一三九, "Foie gras monaka"), then add just enough milk to make it smooth. Sweeten with sugar.

[serving]
Arrange a small amount of the foie gras cream on a dish. Top with a small amount of black fig compote and a fresh fig. Garnish with compote juice.

---

page 一〇五
Rhubarb compote
watermelon, rum jelly and amaretto jelly,
shiso blossom, red *shiso* sprout

[rhubarb compote]
Clean the rhubarb and cut it into pieces. Quickly boil and drain, cook on a residual heat for a while. Marinate it in a sweet vinegar (see page 一三三).

[rum jelly]
   180ml rum
   200g sugar

720ml water

16g gelatin (soften in water)

Mix the ingredients in a pan and heat until the sugar and gelatin are dissolved. Pour into a bowl and cool in an ice water bath.

[amaretto jelly : recommended quantity]

160ml amaretto liqueur

160g sugar

720ml water

16g gelatin (softened in water)

Mix the ingredients in a pan and heat until the sugar and gelatin are dissolved. Pour into a bowl and cool in an ice water bath.

[serving : adequate quantity]

watermelon

shiso blossom

red *shiso* sprout

Place the rhubarb and watermelon in a bowl. Crush both jellies and spoon on top. Sprinkle with *shiso* blossoms and red *shiso* sprouts.

---

page 一〇六

Autumn fruit wrapped in Cointreau flavour

yogurt sherbet

[autumn fruit]

Clean the mascat grape, pear and pomegranate. Cut the pear into bit-size pieces.

[yogurt sherbet]

1kg plain yogurt

200ml milk

250g condensed milk

Mix the ingredients and refrigerate. Stir every hour for a smooth texture.

[cointreau flavoured *kudzu-an* sauce]

45ml cointreau

180ml water

35g sugar

kudzu starch (dissolved with a small amount of water)

Mix and heat all the ingredients except *kudzu* starch in a pan. When the sugar is dissolved, add the mixture of the *kudzu* starch and water, then turn off the heat.

[serving]

Arrange the fruits and yogurt in a bowl and pour the *kudzu-an* sauce.

---

page 一〇七

Kaki compote with cream cheese mousse

black sugar syrup, rum jelly

[*kaki* compote]

kaki (persimmon)

syrup (water 180ml + sugar 100g)

Peel the *kaki* and cut into 8 pieces. Soak in the syrup for one day. (soaking is not necessary, if kaki is ripe)

[cream cheese mousse : serves 8]

100g cream cheese

180ml milk

30g sugar

5g gelatin (softened in water)

70ml fresh cream

Heat the milk, sugar and gelatin in a pan, and turn off the heat when the sugar and gelatin are dissolved. Combine this mixture with the cream cheese and mix in a bowl (don't worry about lumps). Place the bowl in an ice-water bath and mix until it hardens. Add whipped cream and refrigerate.

[rum jelly]

See the rhubarb compote

[serving]

Place the *kaki* compote in a bowl and pour on the brown sugar syrup. Spoon the cream cheese mixture and crushed rum jelly on top.

page 一〇八
Frozen fig with *miso* béchamel

[frozen fig]
Peel the fig and simmer in red wine. Cool then freeze each
fig individually.

[ingredient for *shiro-miso* béchamel]
   250g sweet *shiro-miso*
   béchamel (flour 30g, butter 50g, milk 500ml)
   katsuo-dashi
Mix the sweet *shiro-miso* and béchamel, add an adequate
amount of *katsuo-dashi* and stir until smooth.

[serving]
Arrange the frozen fig in a bowl and pour on the *shiro-miso*
béchamel. Place it in a salamander until slightly seared.

page 一〇九
Beetroot and red wine reduction
milk ice cream, cassis, *shiso* blossoms, *shiso* sprouts

Simmer thinly sliced beetroot in a hibiscus tea.
Combine with the red wine and cassis puree in a pan, add a
red *shiso* sprout, then reduce.
Put milk ice cream in a bowl and place the beets on top
and pour on the sauce. Sprinkle with *shiso* blossoms and
red *shiso* sprouts

神楽坂から神保町、いまは神宮前

神楽坂で修業し、神保町で自分の道を見つけました。移転先の神宮前の店舗はオープンな空間で、料理人のコミュニティの場となることも夢見ています。ジャンルや世代を越えて料理人が交流を深めれば、日本のレストラン文化はもっとおもしろくなる。ここでは毎月近所のレストランと合同スタッフランチの会を開き、外部シェフを招いての協同ディナーも積極的に行なっています。

Our restaurant DEN

In 2016, I moved the restaurant from Jimbocho to Jingumae. The new restaurant has a more free and open atmosphere. We have a monthly luncheon meeting with the staff of the neighboring restaurants and often invite chefs from other fine dining restaurants both at home and abroad, for a collaboration dinner. I hope that DEN will also be a platform of communication for cooks. If the cooks cultivate personal interaction with other categories and other generations, the restaurant culture in Japan will be more interesting.

長谷川在佑
（はせがわ　ざいゆう）
1978 年東京生まれ。
1996 年、東京神楽坂の老舗料亭『うを徳』に入社。
5 年間修業を積む。
2008 年 1 月、東京神保町に『傳』を開業。
2016 年 12 月、店舗を神宮前に移転。

傳
東京都渋谷区神宮前 2-3-18 建築家会館 JIA 館 1F
Tel. 03-6455-5433
https://www.jimbochoden.com

Zaiyu Hasegawa
In 1978 born in Tokyo Japan.
In 1996 chose a culinary career and started working at the traditional
Japanese cuisine restaurant "Uwotoku" in Kagurazaka Tokyo—
trained there for 5 years.
In January 2008 opened the restaurant DEN in Jinbocho Tokyo.
In December 2016 moved DEN to current location Jingumae Tokyo.

DEN
2-3-18 Jingu-mae Shibuya-ku, Tokyo
Tel: 81 3 6455 5433
http://www.jimbochoden.com

傳（でん）　進化するトーキョー日本料理

初版発行　2017 年 11 月 5 日
4 版発行　2025 年 4 月 30 日

著者　　　長谷川在佑

発行者　　丸山兼一

発行所　　株式会社柴田書店
　　　　　東京都文京区湯島 3 丁目 26 番 9 号
　　　　　イヤサカビル　〒113-8477
　　　　　営業部　03-5816-8282（注文・問合せ）
　　　　　書籍編集部　03-5816-8260
URL　　　https://www.shibatashoten.co.jp

印刷・製本　TOPPANクロレ株式会社

ISBN 978-4-388-06273-7